DISCUSSIONS A-Z

INTERMEDIATE

A resource book of speaking activities

Adrian Wallwork

CAMBRIDGE
UNIVERSITY PRESS

CAMBRIDGE UNIVERSITY PRESS
Cambridge, New York, Melbourne, Madrid, Cape Town, Singapore, São Paulo, Delhi

Cambridge University Press
The Edinburgh Building, Cambridge CB2 8RU, UK

www.cambridge.org
Information on this title: www.cambridge.org/9780521559812

First published 1997
12th printing 2007

Printed in the United Kingdom at the University Press, Cambridge

A catalogue record for this publication is available from the British Library

ISBN 978-0-521-55981-2 Resource Book

Contents

Acknowledgements

I would like to dedicate this book to my Macintosh and to all my students who were a great inspiration behind this project. The following people in particular came up with some really good ideas, gave me interesting pieces of information and suggested various books to read: Massimo Malcontenti, Francesco Marconi, Giovanni Mandorino (and all at Tecsiel), Guja Vallerini (and all at Intecs), Maria Turchetto (known to her cult followers as the Great Turchett), Paolo Ghiretti (legal eagle), Rita Sacchelli, Marco Delato, Antonella Pasotto, Giulia Gestri, Antonella Giani, the Giuliani family, the Marino family, Marina Calafà, Isabella Sbrana, Luca Belloni, Elisabetta Marchetti, Ilaria Merusi, Cristiana Toccafondo, Emanuela Ghisolfi, Luca Ferrami (musical inspiration), Luciana Fusar Poli (medical consultant), Giovanni Cozzi, Barbara Bargagna, Monica Ciampi, Paolo Bassi, Andrea Ceccolini, Carlo Bellanca, Claudia Rege Cambrin, Luca Zamboni, Sergio Marchetti, Guido Coli (and all at LIST), Gianluca Soria, Patrizia Caselli (and all at SIAS). Thanks also to LIST SpA for technological support, to International House in Pisa, in particular Chris Powell, Paola Carranza, Lynne Graziani and Antonia Clare, and to Tau Pei Lin, Honor Routledge and Acayo Marcheline Lam for their voices and ideas. A special dedication to Adele Tulloch for giving me a social conscience, and thanks and love to Andreina Marchesi, Tommaso Wallwork and all my family, and to Rupert Burgess and Tom Southern.

I would also like to thank the following people at Cambridge University Press: Jeanne McCarten, Geraldine Mark, Nóirín Burke and Isabella Wigan.

Particular thanks are due to the following institutions and teachers for their help in testing the material and for the invaluable feedback which they provided: David Barnes, The British Institute of Florence, Italy; Jon Butt, International House, London; Bob Hastings, Eurolingua, Córdoba, Spain; Marianne Hirtzel, I.L.A., Cambridge; Anne McKee and Sue Noel, Chambre de Commerce, Pontoise, France; Tony Robinson, Eurocentres, Cambridge; Michael Turner, Chelsea and Holborn School, Barcelona, Spain.

The author and publisher are grateful to the following individuals and institutions who have given permission to use copyright material. It has not been possible to identify the sources of all the material used and in such cases the publisher would welcome information from the copyright owners. HarperCollins Publishers for the extracts on p. 17 from *The Healing Power of Colour* by Betty Ward and the extract on p. 29 from *Sociology* by Haralambos; Little Brown & Co (UK) for the extract on p. 19 from *The Colour of Love* by Y. Alibhai-Brown; Margaret Pauffley for the illustration on p. 19; Popperfoto for the photographs on pp. 19, 51 and 65; excerpt on p. 25 from *1984* by George Orwell, copyright 1949 and renewed 1977 by Sonia Brownell Orwell, reprinted by permission of The Estate of the late Sonia Brownell Orwell, Martin Secker and Warburg Ltd and Harcourt Brace and Company; Time Life Syndication for the extract on p. 31 from Time Magazine, 17 June, 1991; Oxford Cartographers for the maps on pp. 34 and 35; Addison-Wesley Longman for the extract on p. 35 from *The Peters Atlas of the World* by Professor Peters; *The Economist* for the extract on p. 35 from *The Economist*, 25 March, 1989; De Geïllustreerde Pers BV, Amsterdam for the extracts on pp. 43 and 92 from *The World of Wonder*; Stampa Alternativa (Collona Mille Lire) for the extracts on pp. 42 and 43 from *Papalagi* by Tuiavii di Tiavea; The Red Cross for the extracts on pp. 50 and 51; Focus for the extract on p. 55 from *Focus*, February 1995; Guinness Publishing for the extracts on pp. 60 and 61 from *The Guinness Book of Numbers*; The Trustees of G.P. Wells Deceased for the extract on p. 65 from *A Short History of the World* by H.G. Wells; Transworld Publishers (UK and Commonwealth rights) and Writers House Inc. (US and Canada rights) for the extract on p. 65 from *A Brief History of Time* by Stephen Hawking; The Ancient Art & Architecture Collection for the photographs on pp. 67 and 85; Telegraph Publications for the extract on p. 69 from *The Best of Peter Simple*, © 1984; The Continuum Publishing Group for the extract on p. 77 from *Gurdjieff: Essays and Reflections on the Man and His Teaching*; Millfield, Somerset for the extract on p. 77 from their school prospectus; Panos Pictures for the photographs on pp. 79 and 101; Virgin WH Allen plc for the extract on p. 85 from *The Art of Living* by Princess Beris Kandaouroff; Mark Read/Time Out for the photograph of Big Ben on p. 85; Patina for the Swatch on p. 85; Piatkus Books (UK and Commonwealth rights) and Dr Lillian Glass (US and Canada rights) for the extract on p. 93 from *Confident Conversation*; Brinbo Books for the illustration from *Take a closer look* by Keith Kay on p. 95; Plenum Publishing Corporation for the extract on p. 97 from *Sex Roles, Vol. 26*, May 1992; William Heinemann Ltd (UK rights), HarperCollins Publishers (Australia and New Zealand rights) and Simon & Schuster (US and Canada rights) for the extract on p. 99 from *How to Win Frinds and Influence People* by Dale Carnegie; Ravette for the extract on p. 101 from *The Xenophobe's Guide to the English*; Rogers, Coleridge & White Ltd, 20 Powis Mews, London W11 1JN for the extract on pp. 101 and 102 from *My Beautiful Launderette* by Hanif Kureishi © 1986; Little, Brown and Company for the extract on p. 103 from *A Long Walk to Freedom*, © 1994, Nelson Roliblshla Mandela; Sally and Richard Greenhill for the photograph on p. 109; Solo Syndication Ltd for the extract on p. 111 from *The Daily Mail*, February 15, 1993; Respect For Animals for the illustration on p. 11.

Illustrations by Dave Bowyer: pp. 15 (top), 25, 41, 57, 63, 71; Graham Cox: pp. 13, 15 (bottom), 37, 43 (top), 45, 47, 59, 73, 75, 87 (bottom), 89, 105, 107; Gary Wing: pp. 9, 11, 12, 23, 39, 43 (bottom), 49, 65, 81, 83, 87 (top), 91, 93, 95, 97.

Introduction

Summary for those in a hurry

- **Structure:** There are 26 topic-related units – one for each letter of the alphabet. Topics overlap between units, which means that you can pass from one unit to another giving your students a sense of thematic continuity.
- **Level and use:** 'Intermediate' covers an incredibly wide spectrum of levels. You may find that you have to skip some exercises (e.g. some of the listening and reading passages) as they may be too difficult for your intermediate class. This shouldn't, however, mean that you can't proceed with the discussion – the discussion questions which follow the reading passages don't presuppose having read the text itself. Use the book both for back-up material to your coursebook, or independently as the basis for a conversation course. Nearly all of the exercises can also be exploited with more advanced classes.
- **Choosing exercises:** Don't feel you have to do every exercise from every unit. Combine exercises from various units as you choose both from this book and from *Discussions A–Z Advanced* (which has many exercises that can be exploited at lower levels too). Don't follow the order of the exercises unless you want to (or unless advised in the teacher's notes), though you might like to begin with the first exercise in **Appearances** and end with the **Fun with English** section in **English**. Use the **Subject index** and **Links index** to find related exercises in other units.
- **Timing:** Exercises vary in length from five to about ninety minutes depending on your students' level and interest in the topic. Don't impose any rigorous time limits unless you have to, but don't persevere with a discussion that's getting nowhere. However, it is important that students feel they have completed an exercise and been linguistically productive in the process.
- **Personalisation:** Try and relate exercises to current events and things relevant to your own students' lives.
- **Taboo:** Some topics may be sensitive for your students – they are marked with a 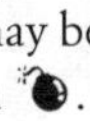. Don't let this put you off doing them unless you're sure they will react badly. If you think they might, make sure you have back-up material ready (for example, exercises from the **Quizzes** or **You** units).
- **Discussion groups:** Most of the discussion exercises work best in pairs or small groups. Explain to students that you won't interrupt them while they talk (unless you notice them repeatedly making the same mistake), but that you'll note down mistakes they make for analysis at a later point. In any case, before embarking on an exercise you should anticipate any vocabulary and grammar problems that are likely to arise, and revise these beforehand if necessary. With more reticent classes you may need to drill or feed them with relevant structures useful for the specific discussion task.
- **Other uses:** Don't think that you have to use this book just for discussions. Some ideas could lead you on to other areas: vocabulary, grammar, composition writing, etc.
- **Flexibility:** Be flexible. Choose your own path through the book. Select and adapt the tasks to suit your students' needs. Rework the exercises or use them as models for your own ideas.
- **Comments:** Please write to me at Cambridge and let me know your opinions and criticisms on the book, or e-mail me: adrian@list.it.

Speaking

Most exercises on the student's page consist of a set of questions to discuss. When these questions are preceded by an introductory reading passage they should not be treated as comprehension questions but as a springboard to discussion. If you see no logical ordering in the numbering of the questions let students read all the questions, and then just select the ones they wish to discuss. Alternatively divide students into small groups and ask them to discuss only the first five of ten questions, for example. Those who finish their discussion quickly can be asked to move on to the other questions, whilst the more loquacious groups are given enough time to finish their debates.
Don't let students think they have to stick to answering the questions directly. Let them float around the questions and bring in their own ideas.
Questions not discussed in the lesson can be set as titles for compositions for homework; or written summaries can be made of those questions that were answered during the lesson.

Reading

Most of texts are authentic and come from a variety of sources; some have been condensed or slightly modified. They have been kept deliberately short and are *not* designed to develop specific reading skills. Encourage students to guess:

- where the texts come from – newspapers, scientific journals, women's magazines, letters, interviews, literary works.
- why they were written – to inform, instruct, convince, advise, shock, amuse, deceive.
- who they were written for – age group, sex, nationality, specialist, casual reader.
- when they were written (where applicable).

Although the aim of the text is not to act as a comprehension exercise, students should obviously understand most of what they read. Before photocopying, underline in pencil any parts that you feel are essential for an understanding of the text. Check the meaning of these before going on to look at the text in more detail.

Introduction

Depending on the type of text, as a written follow-up, students can:

- rewrite the text from a different point of view.
- imagine and recount what happened either before or after the event described in the text. Alternatively they can write up an interview with the people mentioned in the text. This interview could even take place ten years later, to find out their new situations or feelings.
- summarise the text, or simply delete any words or phrases that they consider could be redundant.

Listening

The listening exercises vary in level to a much greater extent than the reading and speaking exercises and can be used with a good range of classes. These exercises are also designed to provide information and provoke discussion, though some listenings can also be used as free-standing exercises to improve listening skills.

None of the listenings are referred to on the student's pages so you should give clear instructions for the exercises. You will also need to dictate the comprehension questions, or write them on the board for students to copy. Feel free to adapt the questions or invent your own to suit the level or interests of your students. Pre-teach any essential vocabulary that has not already come up during the preceding discussion exercise.

Some listening exercises feature native speakers doing the exercise on the student's page. Ask students to read all the questions but without answering them. Then get them to listen to the first two speakers. On the first listening they identify which point is being discussed. After the second listening elicit the structures and vocabulary used – this will then serve as a basis for the students' own discussions. The other speakers can then be used at the end of the exercise, purely as a comprehension test.

Culture and maturity

I am English, but you will notice that there is a considerable American input too. Most of the subjects covered thus reflect a fairly liberal Anglo-Saxon background, and my age (born 1959). Some subjects may encroach on taboo areas in your students' culture and you should take care to consult students in advance about any potentially delicate topics where they might feel embarrassed or exposed. A very simple way to check possible problem areas, is to give each student a copy of the **Subject index** (page 112) and get them to tick any subjects they would feel uneasy about. I would also get them to write their name, so that you know exactly who has problems with what. This means that such subjects could be discussed in such people's absence. This is a good introductory exercise in itself, and should get your students analysing what verbal communication is all about. Also, check out any extreme or prejudiced opinions your students may have; whilst these could actually be used to good effect (as a kind of devil's advocate), they might upset other students.

Don't attempt subjects that are simply outside the realm of your students' experience – no amount of imagination is going to be able to surmount the problem. If you ask them to pretend to be part of a doctors' ethics committee, they can't be expected to know what a real doctor would do, but that shouldn't stop them saying what they would do if they were in such a position.

If you do unwittingly embark on an exercise which students find too difficult or embarrassing, or which promotes little more than uneasy silence, just abandon it – but try and predict such events and have back-up exercises at the ready. Feel free just to ignore some exercises completely, but tell students that the nature of the book is not to cover every exercise systematically and in order. You'll soon learn the types of exercises that will go down well with your students. I would suggest letting the *students* decide which exercises they want to do.

Most exercises in this book have been designed to be very flexible, and an exercise that might appear to be too difficult or delicate can often be adapted to suit your students' needs. In countries where students are likely to seize on a writing exercise, however brief the writing, and use it as a substitute for speaking rather than a prelude to it, you may need to rethink some of the exercise instructions. For example, imagine that students are asked to rate some moral values from one to five according to unacceptability. Don't let them get hold of their pen and merely write numbers, but give them clear-cut instructions which they can't avoid talking about: 'Look at the situations below and decide if they are wrong. If they are wrong, *how* wrong are they? Tell your partner what you think and give reasons for your opinion'. (I am indebted to Jonathan Beesley of the British Council in Kuala Lumpur for these and other suggestions.)

If you feel students cannot cope with a certain exercise because they wouldn't know what to say, then you might have to provide them with a concrete stimulus. For example, students are asked to answer the question 'What difficulties do homeless people have?' If they have difficulty in putting themselves in other people's shoes, you could put them into pairs – one journalist and one homeless person – and give them role cards. On the journalist's card you specify areas to ask questions about (e.g. sleep, food, clothes, money, friends – but in a little more detail than this). On the homeless person's card put information that could answer such questions (e.g. sleep under a bridge, at the station, hospice, etc.). Alternatively, in pairs again, they imagine they are both homeless people, but from two different parts of the world (e.g. New York and Calcutta). By giving them such obvious differences (climate, lifestyle, culture), you get them focusing their ideas more clearly. This principle can be applied to many of the exercises.

Introduction

How to conduct a discussion

The word 'discuss' originally meant to 'cut' with a similar origin as 'dissect'. This meaning, along with its current use of 'examining the pros and cons' gives a good idea of what a discussion is all about, i.e. a dissection of an argument into various parts for analysis, followed by a reassembling of all the relevant elements to a draw a conclusion from the whole. *Discussions A–Z* is based on this principle.

One problem with **question answering** is that without some coaching on *how* to answer questions, students may simply answer 'yes', 'no', 'it depends', etc., and then move on to the next question. Many of the questions in this book have been formulated so that they avoid a simple 'yes/no' answer – but others are designed to be deliberately provocative.

Consider the following case. Students are asked whether it should be up to the government or the people to decide on where people can smoke. If students simply answer 'the government' or 'the people', there won't be much to discuss.

Alternatively, students (either alone or in groups) should first write down a set of related questions, e.g. Where are smokers free to smoke now? Why do we need to change this? Why do we need a law to tell us we can't smoke in certain places? Who would object to anti-smoking legislature? Who would benefit? What should be done with offenders? etc. The process of formulating and answering these types of questions will get the students really thinking, and along with some examples from their own personal experience, should lead to intense language production.

The same kind of approach can be used for **brainstorming**. Suppose you're brainstorming the students on the ideal qualities of a judge. Without any prior instruction, most people will come up with personality characteristics such as intelligent, well-balanced, rational, experienced – which is fine. But it would be more productive if students first wrote down a set of questions related to judges: Why do we need judges? What is a judge? How old should he be? Even the phrasing of questions can be indicative of how we see a judge – why do we refer to a judge as 'he' and not 'she'? Are men more rational, and therefore better judges than women, and why is it that there are so few female judges? You should add other, less orthodox questions, to provoke your students into thinking about other aspects of being a judge, e.g. how relevant are race, height and physical appearance, hobbies etc.? Students may think that the height of a judge is totally irrelevant – this is probably true (though some research has shown that there is a link between height and intelligence) – but often by saying what is *not* important we get a clearer idea of what *is* important. As a follow-up activity students could design a training course for judges.

Now let us see how we can apply the same approach to **problem-solving** activities. Suppose your students are part of a government board which gives funding to scientific research projects. Their task is to decide which one of the following projects to give money to: (1) a group of marine archaeologists who have found Atlantis; (2) some alchemists who have found a way to convert the Grand Canyon into gold; and (3) some genetic engineers who have developed a way to produce square fruit. In order to generate a valuable discussion students should begin by writing down a series of related questions: Why did the scientists propose the projects? Is there a real need for such a project? Is it practical? Do we have the necessary technology to carry it out? Should such projects be funded by the government or by private enterprise? Who would benefit and why? etc. Then, when they are into their discussion, they should try and extend their arguments and reasoning and see where it takes them.

For example, a discussion on Atlantis might, if pre-questions have been written, lead naturally into an analysis of what we can learn from history, how and why legends arise, why archaeology of any kind is important, what things we can learn from past civilizations, how our past effects the present, etc.

In summary, this approach to discussion involves:

- A pre-discussion activity where students, either in groups or individually, write down related questions, some of which you, the teacher, can feed.
- A discussion initiated by answering such questions, and if possible drawing on students' own personal experiences.
- The logical or illogical extension of ideas brought up by the discussion.
- A round-up of conclusions involving cross-group questioning followed by whole class feedback.
- A written summary for consolidation.

The result is obviously a much fuller and productive discussion, in which you have more time to note down any recurrent mistakes, and students to let themselves go and practise their English. Nor are the benefits solely linguistic: there is a great deal of satisfaction in having your mind stretched and producing interesting and often unexpected ideas and results.

Appearances

Warm-ups

- **NB** This exercise could be used for the first lesson with a new group.
- Before you introduce yourself to the class, write the following on the board (which you may need to adapt or add to depending on your particular case):
  My name is X. In groups of four try and answer the following questions. Your answers will obviously be based on my appearance alone. **1** Am I English, American, Australian? **2** How old am I? **3** Am I a teacher, a researcher, a tourist? **4** Am I married, single, other? **5** What do I like doing in my free time? **6** What kind of music/films/books do I like? **7** Am I an introvert or an extrovert? **8** Am I rich or poor? **9** What star sign am I? **10** What religion am I?
- Give students a few minutes to reach their conclusions, then ask individuals from each group to give their answers plus an explanation of how they reached this conclusion. Then give them the answers.

- Onto an A4 page paste two sets of ten or more passport size photos of different people, one set for each sex. Photocopy the page. Put students in pairs and give each a photocopy. They each choose one photo from each set and ask each other questions to find out which photo their partner has chosen.

- Find photos of two similar looking people, alternatively use before and after slimming or baldness photos, typically found in glossy magazines. Give pairs of students one photo each and tell them how many differences they have to find. They then decide if their photos are of the same person or not. They should do this by asking questions, not merely by describing their pictures.

1 First impressions

- Before beginning the exercise, in groups students discuss how they make their initial judgements of people, i.e. before they speak. What things do they then look or listen for? Do they agree that people form 90% of their opinion of someone in the first 90 seconds? Now do the listening.

Listening

- Students hear five people talking about the people on the student's page. First get students to read the ten situations. Then play the tape once. Students' task is to match the situation with the person the speakers are talking about. Play the tape again and elicit some expressions which students can then use in their own discussion.

1*d* **2***e* **3***b* **4***i* **5***c*

1 Because only bad women, they, use heavy make-up to attract men, so that's why we would consider them immoral.
2 Well, I would be put off immediately by a man with long hair at that age, because in the first place I don't like men with long hair, and I would feel that he grew up at a time when it was the normal thing for men to have short back and sides, and the fact that he'd grown his hair would make me think he was trying to look younger than he was.
3 Where I grew up in Uganda, there were lots of Muslim ladies who would wear rings on their nose and earrings.
4 I think I'd be really interested to talk to someone who's got a lot of tattoos to find out the story behind each tattoo, find out why they did it and what it means for them.
5 Well, I have the impression that they're somebody who isn't always thinking about themselves, not looking at themselves in the mirror every morning shaving.

- Students now choose five of questions **a–j** and write an answer. In pairs they read out these answers and their partner has to guess which question was being answered. They then discuss their answers.

Writing

- Students choose one of the following titles: (a) You can't judge someone by their clothes. Discuss. (b) Write a story which begins: 'I couldn't have been more wrong about Jo. The first time I met her she seemed so ...' (c) What would tell you more about a stranger's character: their bathroom cabinet, bookshelves, record collection or wardrobe?

2 Beauty and the beast

- Do a quick class check to verify whether students think that beauty is subjective. Bring in pictures of famous actors and actresses. Students discuss the pictures and then define what being attractive or beautiful is. Are they still sure that beauty is purely subjective? In their groups they then discuss questions **3–6**.
- Use questions **7–12** as a basis of a short whole class discussion (they are designed as a preview to the reading exercise which should either confirm or discredit what came out in the discussion).

Appearances

1 First impressions

It is only shallow people who do not judge by appearances.
The true mystery of the world is the visible, not the invisible.
Oscar Wilde

Fact: People form 90% of their opinion of someone in the first 90 seconds.

What conclusions can you draw from the following information?

a A man who wears an earring in one ear.

b A woman with an earring in her nose.

c A man with a beard or moustache.

d A woman who wears heavy make-up.

e A 60-year-old man with long hair.

f Someone who wears lots of jewellery.

g Someone who's always laughing.

h Someone who bites their nails.

i Someone who has tattoos.

j Someone with red hair.

2 Beauty and the beast

'Beauty is in the eye of the beholder.'

1 Do you think this proverb is true or are there certain norms of beauty?

2 Are we born with an innate sense of beauty or do we acquire it?

3 Is physical attractiveness easier to identify and more important in women or men?

4 Do most people overestimate or underestimate their own beauty?

5 What influence does someone's physical appearance have on their personality? And vice versa?

6 Is beauty only a physical quality?

Aristotle said that beauty was a greater recommendation than any letter of introduction. Which of the following do you agree with?

If you're good-looking you're more likely to:

7 have a pleasant personality and have more friends.

8 study humanistic/artistic subjects.

9 be treated more leniently if you're in the wrong.

10 get a job with higher status.

11 find a partner and get married.

12 be generally happier.

Interesting facts

- University professors often give good-looking girls better marks in exams; male students tend to overestimate the intellectual qualities of pretty female students.
- In court cases attractive people get lighter sentences, unless they made conscious use of their beauty to get their own ends, in which case they might be more severely punished.
- Attractive people are seen by others as having a better personality, higher status, more likelihood of getting married, and being happier.
- Beautiful girls rarely become scientists; they tend to choose subjects such as languages, law and medicine.
- Women who have beautiful bodies often have less self-confidence – they worry too much about keeping their body perfect.
- Short men are less likely to get jobs than tall men and they receive lower starting salaries. In US presidential elections, the taller candidate nearly always wins. There may even be a connection between height and intelligence, as it seems that the same genes are involved in both aspects.

Appearances

3 Make-up

- Students answer the questions in groups and then decide whether make-up actually improves the way we look. To help them decide, find some 'before and after' make-up magazine photos and see if students agree on the value of the transformation.

In a psychological study in the US, male and female subjects were given pictures of women with and without make-up. Both the males and females judged the women to look more physically attractive with make-up on. Men believe that women who wear make-up are more interested in the opposite sex than those who don't; though for most women make-up has simply become a social convention with no sexual connotations.

Listening

- Students hear some facts about the history of make-up. Their task is to put the pieces of history in chronological order, matching them to the illustrations. You may need to pre-teach some of the vocabulary.

4a 5b 3c 1d 2e

1 Make-up was then used to hide the ravages caused by smallpox, and men took to covering their faces with rouge and their heads with masses of false hair. After the French Revolution, a natural look became fashionable and under Queen Victoria, women who used rouge were considered immoral.

2 This century has of course seen an unprecedented rise in all forms of cosmetics, including surgery to remove various blemishes and scars, or purely for vanity. It's interesting that the use of make-up has to some extent turned full circle; young people today often use make-up for some kind of magical effect, and tattoos too are very popular.

3 It seems strange to us now but women in the Middle Ages, well at least in Europe, actually tried to make their skin look even whiter. They did this with flour powder, but anyway they can't have been very dark in the first place; what with their poor diet and the gloomy castle surroundings, they must have ended up looking like an oval, white egg. Later on French women began to paint their faces white, and their lips and cheeks red.

4 Originally in the very primitive tribes only men painted themselves. They lived in terror of evil demons which might harm them when they went out to hunt. They painted grotesque designs on their faces as a disguise, so that the evil demons wouldn't recognise them. Women, who stayed inside the protection of the village, needed no paint of course.

5 Cleopatra was supposed to have painted her brows and lashes black, top lids deep blue and lower lids bright green; she must have looked quite something. It seems incredible but many cosmetics sold today to restore youthful beauty originated from the Egyptian habit of mummifying the dead.

4 Keeping up appearances

- In a multilingual class brainstorm what is acceptable in the students' native countries. As a quick follow-up students write if they would do more of these things in other public places – e.g. parks, cinemas, beaches?

Listening

- Students hear someone saying which of the things she would and wouldn't do. The students' task is simply to write yes or no against the appropriate item, and if possible her reasons.

9 *no* **5** *no* **4** *no* **2** *sometimes* **7** *yes* **8** *no*

I wouldn't spit. I think that's really horrible when people spit on the streets. I wouldn't take my clothes off because you'd probably get arrested. I wouldn't sing because I've got an awful voice. No, I definitely wouldn't sing at the top of my voice. I'd like to say that I wouldn't look at myself in the shop window but I sometimes catch myself just giving a quick glance. I'd wear my pyjamas on the street, I used to do that a lot when I was a student. I wouldn't kiss my partner; I don't like it when people get too affectionate in public places.

Extra

- If you are studying a set text for an examination (e.g. the writing paper in the Cambridge First Certificate in English), students could imagine that the book is being made into a film. Show students pictures of various actresses and actors, and they have to decide who they would choose for the various roles. If there already is a film version, try and find photos of the actors/actresses and mix them with other ones; students can then see if their casting coincides with the real one. Alternatively, students choose from their own classmates, or teachers!

3 Make-up

1 Why do people wear make-up? How do you feel with and without make-up on?

2 How much time do you spend on making yourself up, or on your appearance in general?

3 Do you think you look better with a sun tan? What are the dangers?

4 Why don't men usually wear make-up? If it were socially acceptable would more men wear it?

5 Do you wear perfume or after-shave? Why?

a

b

c

d

e

4 Keeping up appearances

What wouldn't/shouldn't you do in a street?

1 Shout to someone on the other side of the street.

2 Look at yourself in a shop window.

3 Shout at or argue with your partner.

4 Sing at the top of your voice.

5 Take all your clothes off.

6 Eat while walking along.

7 Wear your pyjamas.

8 Kiss your partner.

9 Spit.

10 Cry.

Beliefs

Warm-ups

- Students write down three or four ideas that they associate with the word 'belief', and then a few things that they believe in. In small groups they compare their interpretations of 'belief' and discuss their own beliefs.
- Did students write things like God, ghosts, the evil eye etc., or ideas like democracy, peace? What exactly does believing in something mean? What things did they believe in when they were a child that they don't now, and vice versa? How much have their fundamental beliefs changed in the last 5/10/15 years?

Follow-up

- In groups students invent a strange set of beliefs and rules for a new cult (with a suitable name) that they have supposedly founded. Students then mingle with other groups and try to convince them of their 'beliefs'. Examples: children should not be educated; belief in a sun god and human sacrifice; women should be able to have several husbands; men cannot wear trousers; no laughing; no talking to people older than you unless they speak to you first; men can only walk north-south-north, and women east-west-east.

Writing

- We all need something to believe in. Discuss.

1 isms

- Ask students first to discuss which of the isms express some kind of belief. Then they divide up the isms into three categories of their choice (e.g. beliefs, manias, oddballs, behaviours, social systems). The fact that it is difficult to reduce the categories to three, especially with outsiders such as 'tourism' and 'vandalism' should be a source of discussion in itself. You may find students going off at a tangent and just limiting their discussion to one or two of the isms. Believe it or not there are more than 1250 isms so you may want to write your own list. Here are some more to choose from: ageism, baptism, chauvinism, consumerism, criticism, cynicism, dynamism, escapism, euphemism, heightism, humanism, journalism, mannerism, mechanism, nudism, pessimism, realism, socialism.
- Alternatively, brainstorm students on words that end in -ist. Write these on board. Students then do as above. Finally, they discuss whether they themselves are capitalist, sexist, etc.

Writing

- Students write two sets of definitions for three of the isms. One set should be definitions for children, the second for adults. The definitions should not mention the ism by name. Next lesson, in groups, students read out their definitions; the other members have to guess which ism is being referred to and whether the definition was meant for a child or adult.

2 Superstitions

- Before they look at the questions, ask students (in groups) to invent a 'How superstitious are you?' quiz of around 5 or 6 questions. Change the groupings and get each student to ask the members of his/her new group some of the questions. With less imaginative groups, get students to invent the quiz as a follow-up exercise.
- In the same groups students then try and answer questions **1–5**. Finally, they should try and match the questions with the answers.

⊶ **1** *d* **2** *a* **3** *b* **4** *e* **5** *c*

ⓘ Many of our superstitions probably have their origin in the religious rites and ceremonies of early human settlements. Primitive people needed to make some sense of all the adversities they were subject to – hurricanes, droughts, floods, etc. They believed that there was a connection between such events and some supernatural being or beings. To keep these 'gods' happy they invented a series of rites, which evolved through the various civilisations. In modern times, when salt is actually considered dangerous for health we perhaps forget just how important it was for our ancestors. The word 'salary' comes from the Latin 'salarium' from the word 'sal' meaning salt. The Roman soldiers and civil servants were in fact paid in salt rations and other necessities. The fifth century Goth administrator Cassiodorus said: 'It may be that some seek not gold, but there lives not a man that does not need salt'. In Leonardo da Vinci's picture of the Last Supper, you can see that Judas has accidentally knocked over the salt cellar.

In Roman mythology men had a kind of guardian angel, known as a genius, that looked after their fortunes and determined their character. The genius only existed for men, women had their Juno. Another belief was that everyone had two genii (good and evil), and bad luck was caused by the evil genius.

Follow-up

- Students try and identify from the illustrations which items represent good luck and which bad luck. They should then discuss what brings good and bad luck in their countries.

Beliefs

1 isms

altruism, atheism, cannabalism, capitalism, communism, exorcism, fanaticism, fascism, fatalism, feminism, hedonism, hypnotism, imperialism, materialism, nationalism, optimism, pacifism, racism, sexism, snobbism, terrorism, tourism, vandalism

2 Superstitions

1 Why do some people throw spilt salt over their shoulders?

2 What is the origin of the phrase 'touch wood'?

3 Where does the practice of a 'housewarming' gift come from?

4 Why are black cats supposed to bring bad luck?

5 Why are horseshoes meant to bring good luck?

d

Salt has always been an essential item, in fact many expressions from languages all over the world contain references to salt – the salt of the earth, he's not worth his salt; the Russian term for hospitality is 'khleb-sol' (literally 'bread-salt'), and for the Arabs, eating a man's salt creates a sacred bond. Salt was needed for preserving food so to spill it was a terrible waste and an unlucky omen. This led to the idea that the devil must be standing behind your chair when you spilled the salt. To avert his evil influence the best thing was to throw a pinch of the salt over your left shoulder and into his eye so that he wouldn't be able to see what he was doing.

a

In Greek mythology, when human beings needed assistance they called on their gods, who would then turn them into trees so that they would be protected from their enemies. In Britain certain trees (particularly the oak, hawthorn and willow) were supposed to have sacred powers and these were touched if you wanted to avert bad luck.

e

Black  **cats** have always been associated with witches, they are also difficult to see and are thus associated with evil.

b

This originates from a time when a human sacrifice was made if a new building was being constructed. The victim was buried in the foundations of the building and left to die. Later generations used animals rather than humans, and later still objects were buried rather than animals. In modern times we now bring presents, to keep happy both the owners and the genius who presided over that particular plot of land.

c

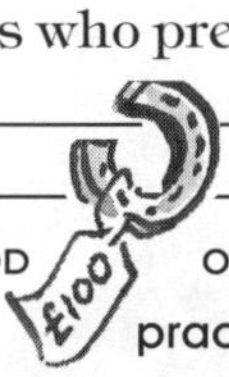

THOR, THE NORSE GOD OF THUNDER, was very fond of iron, and this practice grew in the hope that it would stop him getting angry. Iron was also supposed to have power to keep witches away; in the 17th century nearly all houses had a horseshoe nailed over the threshold.

3 Folklore

- Before reading the passage, in groups students discuss examples of folklore from their own country.
- Students then read the passage. As a whole class get them to imagine how the article might have continued (i.e. an account of cola's powers).

Listening

- Students hear about some of the powers associated with cola. Their task is to tick any of the illustrations which are mentioned in the dialogue.

All of the illustrations are mentioned, in this order: c, e, d, a, f, b

Al Ah.

Su You know if you keep on drinking that stuff you're gonna burn your stomach, it'll give you spots too.

Al Oh don't be ridiculous! I've been drinking cola for years and it's never done me any harm.

Su Well, I had a friend at school and she drank so much it made her throat transparent and split her tongue in two.

Al Yeah right. And I use it to remove the oil from my car.

Su No seriously. Look, you try putting this coin in your glass (yeah), leave it there overnight, and I bet next morning it'll look like new.

Al Ooh! I suppose you use it to remove your nail varnish.

Su How did you guess? (No) I do, really. It's also brilliant for removing stains out of clothes; you can even clean your jewellery too.

Al I remember when I was at college we used to mix it with aspirin, it was supposed to be an aphrodisiac.

Su Did it work?

Al Well, I never had much luck, no.

Su Yeah, well I wouldn't blame that on the cola.

4 Talk to the animals

- Students read the text and then discuss the consequences of the assumptions not being true, e.g. if animals *could* talk what would happen?

3 Folklore

We are often amazed at the incredible things our ancestors believed in, but we rarely stop to think about the things we ourselves now believe in. Stories of *pet baby alligators* being thrown down toilets in New York homes and then reappearing in other people's bathrooms were repeated throughout Europe from the 1960s to the 1990s, with rats taking the place of alligators. Thousands of people swore that they had friends who had been bitten while sitting on the toilet; but these were all merely variations of the same story.

But probably the most universal of folklore beliefs are those associated with the miraculous powers of cola. These may have been inspired by the secrecy surrounding cola's magic formula. ■

a

b

c

d

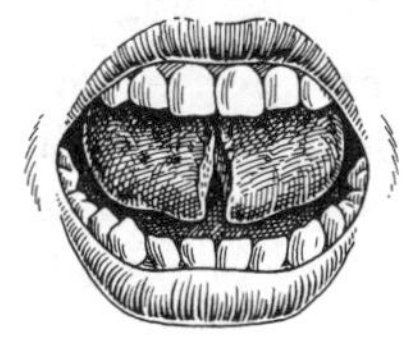

e

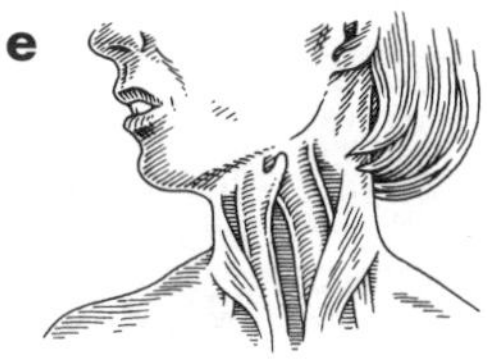

f

4 Talk to the animals

It is not just religion and superstition that is concerned with beliefs. Much of science, for example, is based on a series of beliefs or hypotheses. People used to believe that the earth was flat and the sun revolved around it. They thought madness was a sign of demonic possession and that leeches could be applied to the skin to cure illnesses. But it is not only our ancestors who had some strange ideas. For example, in the 1980s a group of scientists 'discovered' that water has memory.

Here is a list of things that most people believe in. How would it affect our lives if in the future these things were proved to be false?

1 Animals cannot talk.

2 All races are equal.

3 We cannot be in more than one place at the same time.

4 We cannot control the weather.

5 Smoking causes cancer but meat doesn't.

6 There is human life only on the earth.

7 We can only fly with artificial means.

8 We keep the same body and mind for all our lives.

9 We have little control over our dreams and they very rarely come true.

10 Death comes to everyone.

Colour

Warm-ups

- Brainstorm students on the problems of being colour blind. What subjects at school require being able to distinguish colours? What jobs?
- Then get them to imagine how life would be if everything were in black and white. What are the advantages of black and white TV and photos over colour? What do students feel about the colour and layout of their textbooks?

1 What is your favourite colour?

- Students follow the instructions on their page. You may need to pre-teach some vocabulary before students read the texts. When they have finished, tell them the solution. Students then discuss whether there is any truth in the personality descriptions.

1 *black* **2** *blue* **3** *brown* **4** *green* **5** *grey* **6** *orange* **7** *pink* **8** *red* **9** *white* **10** *yellow*

2 Colour chart

- Students fill in the chart and then compare their ideas.
- Discuss colour and fashion, why men and women wear different colours, which colours seem more expensive than others, how the colour of packaging influences our choice of products, etc.

ⓘ The colours we wear have a great influence on our psycho-physical state. A colour is something that can influence our mood, or well-being, and the way we are. This is because colours are partly responsible for the amount of light which gets to our skin and the stimulation our skin derives from it. Food dyes are artificial colours used by food manufacturers to help increase sales of their products. Consumers tend to associate a bright colour with freshness, wholesomeness and tastiness. Laboratory experiments have shown that if a range of drinks is presented with identical flavours, most consumers will report that the more darkly coloured the drinks are, the stronger they appear to taste. Moreover, banana-flavoured drinks dyed red will be reported as having a strawberry flavour. The colour of packaging has significant effects on sales. In 1996 Pepsi began a multi-million dollar campaign and changed its brand colour to blue. One mobile phone group renamed itself Orange.

Listening

- Students listen to a phone-in programme about colour in various aspects of our lives.
Questions: **1** What effect do blue clothes have on the wearer? **2** What colour clothes is caller one wearing? **3** What is caller two worried about? **4** What is the expert's advice for caller two? **5** Why should yellow be avoided in shops? **6** Where might yellow be a good colour and why? **7** How does pink make people feel? **8** Why is red not a good colour for car rear lights? **9** What would be the best colour for fire engines?

1 *calming effect + makes brain more alert* **2** *red* **3** *food dyes and additives* **4** *avoid artificial dyes* **5** *encourages stealing* **6** *restaurants – speeds up eating* **7** *lethargic* **8** *gives impression of being further away than it really is* **9** *yellow*

P = presenter R = Rosie C = caller

P Tonight on Kaleidoscope we're very happy to have Rosie Brown back with us in the studio. You're going to be talking to us about how to put a little colour in our lives.

R Yes, Derek, and you look as if you could do with some, you're rather pale aren't you?

P Well I'm cooped up in the studio all day – anyway let's hear the first caller's question.

C1 Er, yes yes, I would like to know if the colour of your clothes has any effect on the way you feel.

P Well, Rosie's wearing blue tonight, any reason for that Rosie?

R Actually Derek there is. Blue helps you calm down in nervous situations, like erm radio interviews, and also makes your brain more alert. Can I just ask what colour the caller is wearing?

C1 Yes, I wear a lot of red, which is actually what I'm wearing now.

R Red's a good colour if you want to help your blood circulate, it also stimulates physical activity but is not much use if you need to focus your concentration on something particular.

P OK. Let's move on to caller two. Can we have your question please?

C2 Em, I've got two young children and I'm getting rather worried about all those dyes and additives in their food.

R There's quite a lot of controversy around food dyes. Some doctors I know say they can be the cause of all kinds of things – hyperactivity, asthma, headaches, even eczema. My advice would be to avoid them, at least the artificial ones. But of course there are natural food dyes, and if you're a cook, you may know that the Mexicans used to dye some of their foods with tints obtained from the dried bodies of insects.

P Oh yuck! Sounds revolting. Anyway we've got another caller on line four.

C3 I'm going to be opening a clothes shop quite soon and I wondered if Rosie could recommend any colours.

R Well, I'm not sure I could recommend any particular colour, I think that's such a personal thing, but what I can do is to tell you what to avoid and that's yellow.

P Yellow?

R Yes, studies have shown that yellow actually makes people want to steal things.

P Is that so?

(Tapescript continued on p. 18)

Colour

1 What is your favourite colour?

Your favourite colour can tell you a lot about your *personality*

If it is either brown, black, or blue, read 1–3, orange, green or grey, read 4–6, red, white, pink, or yellow, read 7–10. Decide which description best fits you.

1 Want to give impression of mystery; sophisticated, dignified and impressive; always wearing this colour indicates protest.

2 Deliberation, introspection, conservatism, duty; like to be part of a group; good mixer, affectionate and faithful; loyal friends; sometimes inflexible beliefs, worrier.

3 Solid, substantial, good worker; patient, conscientious, dutiful, dependable, responsible; not impulsive, obstinate in habits; don't like change.

4 Frank, community-minded, hopeful, a little moralistic; too self-effacing, modest and patient thus easily exploited; too much of this colour indicates high level of anxiety.

5 Cautious, searches for composure and peace, dedicated; may turn away from worldly things but have business ability, works too hard; compromises.

6 Colour of luxury and pleasure; flamboyant and fun-loving; inclined to dramatize; generally good-natured and popular; curious, maybe superficial.

7 Love and affection without passion; charming and gentle; a little indefinite; extreme fondness of this colour indicates desire for protection, special treatment and a sheltered life.

8 For those who are or want to be out-going; vigorous and impulsive, determined, optimistic; not very objective or aware of shortcomings.

9 Pure, innocent, naive but lively and well-balanced personality; worn continuously suggests immaturity and idealism.

10 Happy, wise, imaginative, mentally adventurous; good in business, intellectual, clear thinker; can be rather stubborn and opinionated. ◆

2 Colour chart

category		best colour	worst colour
car	family-type		
	luxury (e.g. Rolls Royce)		
eyes			
shoes			
coat			
house	exterior		
	bedroom		
ice-cream			
toothpaste			

Colour

3 Gentlemen prefer blondes

- Students read the text and answer the questions in groups.

Listening

- Students hear about hair colour habits in the USA and answer these questions.
  Questions: True or False? **1** There is a higher percentage of blonde women pictured in magazines than there is in real life. **2** About 25% of the white population in the US is blonde. **3** Many US college students would like to be blonde. **4** Most US men prefer their women blonde. **5** Only 13% of US men prefer red-heads.

1 *T* **2** *T* **3** *T* **4** *F (brunettes)* **5** *F (14%)*

Su Wow! I like the hair Jo. Blonde, is that your new look?
Jo Yeah, I fancied a change, and do you know what, I feel really attractive too.
Su Em, you've been reading too many fashion magazines.
Jo What do you mean?
Su Well, I've been reading this report that says that there are far more blonde women pictured in certain magazines than there are blonde women in actual life.
Jo You mean a disproportionate number?
Su Yeah, apparently about a quarter of the white population in America are real blondes, but in some men's magazines, for example, and not just men's, well over a third of the women featured are blonde.
Jo Well, they do say that gentlemen prefer blondes.
Su You're so frivolous sometimes, aren't you Jo? Don't you see that this has important implications?
Jo Like what?
Su It means that women like you are conditioned into dyeing their hair blonde, because they think it makes them more attractive. They did some survey of white college students and discovered that although only around a fifth were actually natural blondes, thirty nine per cent wished that they were.
Jo I think you take these things too seriously.
Su Well, be that as it may, the funny thing is that although nearly all these girls thought that men preferred blondes, actually only a third do, over a half preferred brunettes.
Jo And what about the poor redheads like you?
Su A measly fourteen per cent.
Jo Ah, now I understand why you've got it in for my blonde hair.

4 Skin deep?

- Students read the text which is an extract from an interview with a white woman, Sue, who married a black man, and had children, by him. She recounts how white people abuse her when she takes her daughter, Esme, out for walks, and how even her mother, Jenny, has rejected her. It is important for them to understand exactly how Sue and her mother feel (i.e. almost ashamed to have a black [grand]child); so get some feedback from students on this. Students then discuss the questions.
- Put students in pairs – S1 plays the part of Sue, and S2 Jenny her mother. They should act out a dialogue in which Sue confronts her mother with her (the mother's) racial prejudices. The mother should try and give some justification for the way she feels and Sue should explain how wrong these explanations are.
- Alternatively, S1 plays the part of Sue, and S2 Esme her child. S1 has to explain why white people are prejudiced against blacks and the difficulties Esme is likely to have in her life. S2 should try and ask typical child-like questions (i.e. a lot of whys).
- Finally, choose two students to act out their dialogue, and then use this as a basis for a discussion on racism, or alternatively proceed to **Xenophobia** which discusses this subject in more depth.

Tapescript continued from p. 16. **2 Colour chart**

R But yellow's fine if you've got a restaurant, because it encourages people to eat up fast and go. Colour's a funny thing. There was a period when American football clubs used to paint their guest changing room pink, as this was supposed to make the opposition become super-relaxed and so rather lethargic on the field.
P Interesting. Right. We've got time for one more question.
C4 Why is that at the traffic lights I can always see the green better than the red?
R This is an interesting question which brings up a whole host of issues connected with safety. Red has always been associated with danger and thus probably seemed a good choice as a stop at traffic lights and the same reasoning was presumably applied to the rear lights of cars. But scientists have proved that a much more effective colour would be green for the rear lights, especially as red gives the driver behind the impression of being much further away than they really are. Fire engines too would be much better off if they were painted yellow rather than red. But to go back to the caller's question and without wanting to go too far into the technicalities ...

3 Gentlemen prefer blondes

The colour of your skin and hair is genetically determined, and basically depends on how much pigment, mainly melanin, you have. Red-haired people have an additional pigment, and some non-scientific people would argue that this pigment also affects their character, making them irate and aggressive.

People tend to make associations based on hair colour. The media exaggerate this by focusing on certain stars and personalities whose hair in some way reflects the colour of the age or society that they live in. Marilyn Monroe, for example, was responsible for the myth that gentlemen prefer blondes, though Jackie Kennedy gave brunettes a short lived supremacy. The media may also be responsible for making young blacks and Japanese, for example, want to change the colour of their hair.

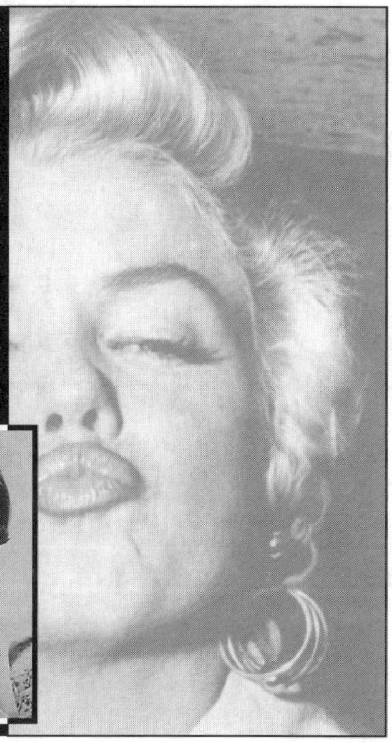

1 What associations with hair colour are made in your country? Are some colours considered to be better than others?

2 Would you ever consider dyeing the colour of your hair? Why do women tend to dye their hair much more than men? Are women influenced more than men by the media?

3 Should races with particular hair characteristics try and change them (e.g. Afro-Americans straightening their hair, Japanese dyeing their hair), or are they denying or undermining their culture? And white people with dreadlocks?

4 Skin deep?

These are my children. How can people see only their race? My mother won't go to the shops with the children. She has asked them to call her Jenny. I know why: it's because she doesn't want them calling her Granny in public.

It is terrible to say this, because I am talking about my own children and I love them, but because I am white, if I'm on my own, I can walk anywhere, I feel free, nobody bothers. But when I have my children with me, I am a prisoner to how people feel about me and the children. I can feel their looks and the prejudices, even when my children can't. And you do want to belong. The first day I went to the nursery, all the white mums started getting together and being pals. Then one of them started being really rude about Blacks – 'Pakis' – and I just froze. For a second I felt just like my mother and hoped that my daughter wouldn't rush up to me at that point.

1 Do you judge people on the colour of their skin? Consciously or unconsciously?

2 Can you sympathise with the speaker? And with her mother?

3 What difficulties do you think there are in being of mixed race (i.e. with parents from different races)?

4 Would you be friends with, have a relationship with, or marry someone from another race?

5 Is there racial discrimination in your country?

Decisions

Warm-ups

- Brainstorm students on the most important decisions one has to make in one's life. Write them on the board, adding any of the following if the students themselves don't come up with them: choosing a school/college/university, choosing friends, leaving home, choosing a life-long partner, deciding to have children, choosing a job, deciding to change job/career, breaking up with partner, moving house/country, changing religion. Now get students to rank the decisions in terms of importance and life-changing impact. Finally, in pairs students discuss the most important decision that they personally have had to make, and the most important decision/s they will have to make in the future.

1 Good and evil?

Students read the passage and answer question **1**. Make sure you get feedback after they've answered question **1**. Most students would prefer to be Juju. If they do prefer Juju, it probably means that they've missed the point. Juju and the king are, to all intents and purposes, the same, in that they both believe that their souls are pure and that they've done nothing wrong. The king is, after all, doing no more than is expected of him – he is acting within the morality of his age, he has no inkling of a doubt that he may be doing something wrong. Students should not judge the king with their own morality, which as question **4** is designed to show, may really be little better than the king's. If you judge the situation objectively, you'd be much better off being the king, who knows he's in the right, and unlike Juju, doesn't suffer.

(**4**) By not helping the people of the third world are we not, to some extent, similar to someone who watches a child drowning in a swimming pool and does nothing to help? This situation is obviously more immediate than helping the starving, but it's difficult to deny that we are not just as aware of what is going on in Africa as we are of someone six feet away from us.

ⓘ This passage comes from the Hungarian novel *The Fifth Seal* by Ferenc Santa. The fifth seal is mentioned in Revelations VI, 9-11: And when he had opened the fifth seal, I saw under the altar the souls of those that had been killed because they had proclaimed God's word and had been faithful in their witnessing. They shouted in a loud voice, 'Almighty Lord, holy and true, how long will it be until you judge the people on earth and punish them for killing us?' On a similar line you might like to read Hopkins' poem *Thou art indeed a just Lord* which contains the line 'Why do sinners' ways prosper?'

2 Dilemmas?

- Students make their choices individually, and then discuss them in groups.

Listening

- Students hear the following alternatives which they have to decide between. Play the pieces several times each. Students write down their answers/gut reactions as they listen, then after all ten have been answered, students discuss them in groups. Decide whether to use all ten questions or not.

1 Which would you rather be – a man or a woman?
2 Would you prefer a year in prison or a year completely alone on a beautiful desert island?
3 Given the choice would you choose not to eat for three days or not to sleep for three days?
4 What do you want – a beautiful house but miles from anywhere or an average house near to everything you want?
5 If you had to spend a month in Siberia or a month in the Sahara, which would you prefer?
6 Imagine this – you can either be incredibly rich but full of regrets and with no hope, or incredibly poor but full of hope.
7 Right. You can either be taller and a little less intelligent or considerably shorter and a lot more intelligent. Which is it going to be?
8 If you could have two weeks visiting ten different towns or two weeks in one particular interesting place, which kind of holiday would you go for?
9 So, you're about to take an important oral exam, let's say an English oral, and you can either wait with someone like you who has yet to do the exam or with someone who's just finished it. Who are you going to wait with?
10 I'm not sure how I'd answer this one myself, but the choice is between a life of permanently following your head or permanently following your heart.

ⓘ (**2**) A study of case histories of people in total isolation, members of religious groups and people who had been shipwrecked, showed some similarities – sudden fearfulness and feelings resembling anxiety attacks. People need other people.

Writing

- Students write an essay describing how their life would have been different if they had been born of the opposite sex.

Decisions

1 Good and evil?

ONCE UPON A TIME on the island of Luch-Luch lived a common slave called Juju. One day his master, the King, asked Juju why he was smiling. Sensing trouble, Juju replied honestly: 'Something came into my mind and made me smile.' The king said, 'Well, I shall see to it that nothing will ever enter into your mind again!' And he had Juju's tongue cut out, thinking that if he deprived the slave of his tongue, he would be disposing of his thoughts as well.

Later Juju's 11-year-old daughter was taken away from him and died serving the king's pleasure. Then he lost his little son to the king. Despite all this pain, Juju consoled himself with the thought that in his whole life he had not committed a crime: 'I did not do things like this to others. Instead, others did them to me. My soul remained as pure as it was at the time of its creation.'

The king lived a life that was the very opposite of the unfortunate Juju's in every possible way. All of Luch-Luch obeyed his every command. In the first decade of his reign he killed 9624 people, he had 2000 people blinded in one eye, and 1500 tongues torn out. But he was convinced that he was the most decent human being in the whole world! His mother thought so too – until he had her beheaded – and so did his children and friends. He didn't suffer the slightest twinge of conscience because he was behaving in accordance with the morality of his epoch.

1 With your partner you have five minutes to decide if you want to be resurrected as the king or Juju.

2 If you overthrew the king, and you became king in his place, what punishment would you give him?

3 Were people like Hitler really evil or just acting as they thought best?

4 When we go to 'heaven' how will we be able to justify the fact that we had cars and VCRs whilst millions of people were starving around us? Why don't you give more money to beggars?

5 Do you believe in some kind of ultimate justice or how else do we explain all the suffering in the world?

2 Dilemmas?

1 Which would you rather lose – your sense of taste or sense of smell?

2 Choose between being extremely ugly and very intelligent, or incredibly beautiful but particularly stupid.

3 Would you prefer to never see your family again, or never see any of your friends again?

4 Would you rather you had twenty exciting eventful years ahead of you, or forty fairly routine years?

5 You can be reborn black or white – which would you choose?

3 Decision-making

- In pairs, students should discuss the situations and what they would do to resolve them.
- Students get into pairs and identify the situation illustrated in the pictures. They then choose one of the situations 1, 3, 4 and 5. S1 plays him/herself, and S2 takes the part of the other person (e.g. the teacher in situation 1, the arrested woman in situation 3, etc.).

4 Papa don't preach

- In groups students decide who should make the decisions – parents or children. They can also prioritise the decisions, i.e. deciding which decisions must be made by, for example, the child, down to those which don't really matter. You might like to divide students up into parents and children; in pairs they then have to argue their case.

Listening

- Students hear two people discussing who they think should decide in some of the situations. Students should identify which point each speaker is talking about and who they choose as the decision-maker in each situation.

1 *e child* **2** *b parents* **3** *d parents* **4** *c children* **5** *g children* **6** *e parents*

1 I was em, I was always allowed home at whatever time I wanted and I really appreciated that, I just used to have to ring up if I was going to be late.

2 I had a TV in my room and I spent the whole of my adolescence watching TV shut in my room; I even took my meals into my room. So I really don't think children should be able to choose that, I think parents ought to set some limits.

3 Em, I think parents should be advising their children on what to read, but you can't control it; in the end children are just going to read what they want.

4 Whenever my parents tried to stop me from seeing particular people it only made me want to see them even more. I think parents should give advice but they should never force you who to see and who not to see.

5 Em, I was very pressurised by my family into becoming a doctor and uh, I had to totally rebel against them in fact after I'd started medical school.

6 I really think parents ought to say what time a child has to come home because a child even at 16 might complain about oh my friends stay out until midnight why can't I, but really you appreciate the limits because you feel they care about you.

3 Decision-making

1 Your English teacher has lost all interest in teaching your class. All you ever do is grammar, reading and listening exercises.

2 Your family has had a grocery store for more than 50 years. Recently, a supermarket has opened 100 metres down the road.

3 You are a police officer and you have just arrested this woman for stealing food from a supermarket. On the way to the police station she tells you that in the previous two weeks she's lost her purse, her dog has been run over and her sister has been involved in a car accident.

4 Your husband/wife suffered a serious car accident a few years ago, and since then has been confined to a wheel chair. You had to give up your job to look after him/her and more recently he/she has become so demanding that you have to spend all your time with him/her.

5 You are pregnant and 45 years old. Your doctor has told you that there is a 50% chance that you will give birth to a child with Down's syndrome.

6 You are a scientist and have discovered a method to improve our intelligence by 500%. It involves injecting the foetus at three months with a liquid which has no side effects. You are (Your partner is) two months' pregnant.

4 Papa don't preach

Who should decide:

a which school to go to and what subjects to study?

b what to watch on TV?

c what friends to have?

d what to read?

e what time to come home at night?

f when and what to eat?

g what job to have?

h whether to have an abortion?

i whether to go to church?

j which political party to vote for?

English

Warm-up

- Ask students to cover the left-hand column of the chart and identify or guess the languages shown in the illustration. They show the present tense of the verb 'to be' in Old English, Latin and Sanskrit.

1 A world language

- Students read the passage and then answer the questions. **NB** This and the following exercise practise various areas of English usage and are designed to get students thinking about differences between their language and English.

Follow-up

- With monolingual students, give them these instructions: Your native language and English have been nominated for adoption as the world language. Imagine that the number of speakers of both languages is the same, and that there are no economic or political advantages of adopting one rather than the other language. The choice of language will therefore depend totally on its ease of learning and its effectiveness in communication. Choose a few areas of your language which you think are better than English.

2 Newspeak

- Students read the passage about Orwell's *1984*. Then, in groups, they imagine that they are members of a board of linguists whose job is to simplify the English language for use in international communication. They think of all the areas of English which they have difficulty in, and how these could be simplified or even eliminated completely. The idea is that students are forced to analyse the necessity for some of the distinctions that exist in English, though within a context that they are likely to find more entertaining. In all cases, students should analyse the uses of the tenses, forms or words in question before deciding which ones to abolish. You can obviously choose other elements to add to the list, if these are areas that are causing your students particular problems. Other elements are dealt with in the follow-up exercise.

Here are some suggestions:
Possible redundant tenses (students choose to eliminate one of the following pairs): present simple / present continuous, going to/will, present perfect/simple past.

Possible redundant words: be/have (some languages don't have a distinction, e.g. Welsh), may/can, make/do, say/tell, talk/speak, bring/take, big/large (little/small), hello/goodbye, because/why, by/from.

Follow-up

- Students imagine a crazy dictator has taken power. He/She has ordered the following changes to the language. The students' task is to assess what differences this would make and what difficulties, if any, it would create: **1** Separate pronouns depending on skin colour. **2** Sentences must be no longer than ten words (except in literature). **3** No words of Latin or Greek origin are allowed. **4** The use of the passive is banned. **5** All prepositions are abolished. **6** Exclamation marks, colons and semi colons are banned. **7** No swear words. **8** No words to contain the combination 'th'. **9** The following words are banned: no, my, the, one, see, come, white, woman. **10** On Wednesdays everyone has to speak in a foreign language.

English

1 A world language

According to a legend, originally the world only had one language. One day the people decided to build an enormous tower so that they could reach up to heaven. The creator, convinced that he had to put an end to such futile ventures, decided to confuse their language so that they couldn't understand each other, and to scatter them all over the earth.

Since that time people throughout the world have been struggling to understand each other.

Most European languages can, nevertheless, be traced back to a single root – Sanskrit.

Modern E	am	are	is	are	are	are
Old E	eom	eart	is	sindon	sindon	sindon
Latin	sum	es	est	sumus	estis	sunt
Sanskrit	asmi	asi	asti	smas	stha	santi

For example the Sanskrit word for *brother* was *bhratar*, which in Irish is *bráthair*, *brat* in Russian, *phrater* in Greek, *Bruder* in German and *broeder* in Dutch.

Despite various attempts to create universal languages – between 1880 and 1907 no less than 53 were invented – today, whether we like it or not, English is the only universal language, apart, that is, from music and love.

1 Are there many words in your language which look or sound similar to English, and which have the same meaning?

2 What English words are regularly used in your language? Why were they borrowed and are they used in the same way as in English? Has their grammatical form been altered in any way? Are they pronounced as in English? Are they accepted by your government or do some linguistic purists want to eliminate them?

3 What words has English borrowed from your language?

4 How do you feel about English being the world language? Do you accept it or do you think there is still a place for Esperanto?

2 Newspeak

In George Orwell's satire, *1984*, a dictatorial political regime invents a new language, Newspeak. The government wants to reduce the complexity of the language and so limit people's ability to think, thereby preventing them from rebelling against the government.

One of the distinguishing marks of Newspeak grammar was its regularity. The simple past of *think* was *thinked*; all such forms as *swam, gave, brought, spoke, taken* etc. were abolished. All plurals were made by adding -s or -es. The plurals of *man, ox, life,* were *mans, oxes, lifes*. Comparison of adjectives was invariably made by adding -er, -est (*good, gooder, goodest*); irregular forms and the *more, most* formation were suppressed.

3 Fun with English

- This is good for a last lesson. Students get into groups and find the appropriate answers. Make it competitive by seeing which group manages to answer the most questions correctly. If you're short of time, only do the first part (questions **1–11**) and forget the listening. Although students may not be familiar with some of the words, they should be able to make some reasonable deductions.

1 *with, eighth, telephone*
2 *abstemious*
3 *fanzine (a magazine for music fans), flexitime (flexible time, i.e. arriving and leaving work to suit yourself), workaholic (someone who is addicted to work, like someone who is addicted to alcohol)*
4 *discotheque, laboratory, gymnasium*
5 *goodbye (cf. farewell = fare you well)*
6 *children, mice, women*
7 *smack, crash, gulp (I found loads of these in Peanuts)*
8 *baby-sitter, knowhow, spaceship*
9 *compact disc (CD), random access memory (RAM), unidentified flying object (UFO)*
10 *Was it ...? Pull up ... (These are known as palindromes.)*
11 *Peter Piper ... Swan swam ...*
12 *He said that that 'that' that that man said was correct. (You could explain this by saying the man had a choice of saying 'which' or 'that' and that 'that' was correct).*
13 *You are too good to me to be forgotten.*
14 *backwards, you*
15 *all American spellings*
16 *ate/late*

Listening

- An English woman is trying to convince an Indian woman that nothing can beat English as a world language. Students' task is to tick off any items from **1–11**, mentioned during the listening. With more advanced students get them to write down any other reasons why the English woman is convinced that English would be a good world language.

8 *(composite words – weekend, skyscraper, playboy, knockout* **10** *(boy, yob)* **9** *(acronyms – WASP)* **7** *(onomatopoeic – snarl etc.)* **3** *(blended words – brunch, smog, motel, cheeseburger)* **4** *(clipped words – ad)* **5** *(plurals – children, mice and women).*

Reasons for English being a world language: only one word for you; word creations (nouns to verbs etc.); no cases; no gender; simple way to create plurals.

A OK so you only have one word for 'you' but what about English spelling and pronunciation? You're not going to tell me that they're easy to learn.
B No, all right, I agree with you there. But apart from that, there's really nothing that can beat English as a world language.
A Convince me.
B Well, look at the ease with which we put two words together and get a totally new one. I mean what's the point of saying 'end of the week' when you can say 'weekend'?
A That's not so original, many languages can do that.
B Yes, but did they give you 'skyscraper', 'playboy', 'knockout'?
A OK. More reasons.
B Name another language in which you can spell a word backwards and get a new word, like boy to yob, b-o-y y-o-b.
A What is a yob?
B An aggressive teenager.
A OK, I like that one. Anymore like that?
B Well, what about the way we make acronyms out of words, like when you take the first letter from a series of words and you get a new one, WASP for instance.
A Wasp?
B Yeah it was all the rage in the States in the late eighties – it stands for White Anglo Saxon Protestant.
A Not sure I like that one.
B Well all right then, try these: snarl, sneer, sneeze, sniff, snivel, snore, snort, snuffle.
A They're not acronyms are they?
B No. No, I was just trying to give you an idea of how good English is at imitating sounds. And what about 'brunch'?
A What about 'brunch'?
B Well, it's two words squashed into one – breakfast and lunch.
A Oh, I hadn't realised that.
B Yeah, apparently Lewis Carroll, you know the one who wrote *Alice in Wonderful*, he coined the first one, and since then we've had 'smog', 'motel' and 'cheeseburger', amongst others. And then we can clip the ends of words.
A What do you mean by that?
B Well we can make a long word shorter by cutting its end off. So instead of saying 'advertisement', which no one knows how to pronounce correctly anyway, we can say 'advert' or even plain simple 'ad'.
A Fine, so English is a fun language, (Yeah) but so far you haven't really given me any concrete or at least good reasons why English is so suitable for being a world language.
B OK let's get serious. English has a unique ability to produce instant new words, because we don't have to worry about endings or whatever, we can convert adjectives into nouns, nouns into verbs, and verbs into adjectives.
A Well, that is useful, I have to admit. But I'm still not convinced.
B You want more? English has no cases or gender, right? You don't have to remember whether something is nominative or accusative, or whether it is masculine or feminine.
A But don't you say 'she' for ships? Cars too, I've heard people saying things like 'She's a really good drive.'
B OK. But they're the exceptions. You want to form the plural? What could be easier than a simple 's'? And you only have to put that on nouns, you don't have to remember to put it on adjectives or whatever.
A Not so simple. What about child children, mouse mice, woman w...?
B Well, again exceptions, yes.
A A lot of exceptions this language of yours.

3 Fun with English

Pull up if I pull up.

abstemious	baby-sitter	CD	child
crash	disco	eigth	fanzine
flexitime	goodbye	gulp	gym
knowhow	lab	mouse	RAM
smack	spaceship	telefone	UFO
whit	woman	workaholic	

Swan swam over the sea;
swim, swan, swim!
Swan swam back again;
well swum swan.

Peter Piper picked a peck of pickled pepper;
a peck of pickled pepper Peter Piper picked.

Was it Eliot's toilet I saw?

Find examples of 1–11 in the boxes above.

1. Three words that are spelt incorrectly.
2. A word that contains all the vowels in alphabetical order.
3. Three words that are a combination of two words squashed together (e.g. brunch = breakfast + lunch). What do you think the words mean?
4. Three words that have been clipped at the end (e.g. advertisement → advert → ad).
5. A very very common salutation that originally meant 'God be with you'.
6. Three words with irregular plurals.
7. Three onomatopoeic words frequently found in comics.
8. Three words which are a composite of two words (e.g. week + end = weekend).
9. Three acronyms (e.g. RADAR = **ra**dar **d**etection **a**nd **r**anging).
10. Two sentences that read the same (letter for letter) forwards and backwards (e.g. Madam, I'm Adam).
11. Two tongue twisters (i.e. sentences that are very difficult to say fast).

Now answer these questions.

12. Punctuate the following sentence: He said that that that that that man said was correct.
13. Decipher the following:

UR	2	GOOD
	2	ME
	2	BE
	<u>4</u>	GOT
	10	

14. Answer the following question: ?*sekatsim gnilleps owt eht tops ouy nac tub sdarwkcab gnidaer ysae yrev ton si ti*
15. What do the following words all have in common? *color, jewelry, program, traveling, theater*
16. Which of the following pairs of words rhyme? *ate/late even/seven here/there, now/know over/cover*

Family

Warm-up

- Brainstorm students on all the English words they can think of to express family relationships (e.g. mother, cousin, aunt etc.). In groups they then think of any distinctions in their own languages which don't occur in English (e.g. no distinction between male and female cousin, no common unique word for brothers and sisters) and vice versa.

The type of kinship words a language has is obviously indicative of how important the family is in that society. Yiddish has a word meaning 'the father of the girl/boy I'm going to marry'. In Neo-Melanesian (spoken in the area around Papua New Guinea) they even distinguish between an 'aunt by marriage' and 'a mother's sister', and between the 'father's brother's child' and 'mother's sister's child'. In Njamal, an Australian aboriginal language, the words for father and uncle are the same; and in Italian they make no distinction between grandchildren and nephews and nieces. Many languages have words to differentiate between an elder brother and a younger brother. Hungarian even distinguishes between 'my elder brother' and 'your elder brother'. As society changes some kinship words fall into disuse as the family bonds they used to express are no longer considered to have important status.

- Students now draw a diagram of their family tree and then discuss it with their partner. Then as a whole class try and decide on a definition for 'family' – this exercise will obviously work better in multinational classes.

1 Family ties

- Students look at the diagrams of family situations, identify which category their own family fits into, and whether this is typical of their country. Then students discuss the pros and cons of each category. Finally they discuss questions **1–6**.

Listening

- Students hear an Indian woman (born in Britain) describing how an Indian family differs from an English family (see question 6 on student's page). Before dictating the questions, get students to predict differences between Indian and English family life.

Questions: **1** Does the Indian woman agree that there is no family life in England? **2** Is the typical English family nuclear? **3** List two pros and two cons of the extended family. **4** Who is expected to look after old people in England?

1 *no* **2** *yes* **3** *pros: support for other family members (young help old), sense of continuum (not fragile like nuclear family); cons: intrusive, no room for individuality, forced to do what you don't necessarily want to do, conservative* **4** *the state*

A It seems a strange thing to be asking really the difference between family life in England and India, because a lot of people would say there is no family life in England. Do you find that? Do you find that there's much of a difference?

B Um, there is a great difference I would say – I think there is a family life in England (A: Oh good) but it's very different – I think that it's essentially, in England, there's a nuclear family basically, you know, and erm, so everyone's lives are geared around their the two parents, let's say, if it's a standard family, and the children (A: yes). In India, it's very, very different, on the whole. There are – it's an extended family, and so therefore in any one house you will often get grandparents, you know then the parents, then the children. And in this way, the lifestyle is very different because everyone has a say in everyone's life. And also there's lots of support there as well ...

A ... Do you think that ... I mean ... this sort of extended family is a sort of a continuing thing isn't it? I mean the fact that there are so many people of such different ages in it, and that when one person dies, other people are born in, and it goes on and on (B: it goes on an' on absolutely) – it's a continual thing. Whereas a nuclear family can be such a fragile thing, an isolated thing, it's a fragile thing (B: very much so), it can fall apart so easily.

B It's hard, there are pros and cons, I mean, in India, you know, because it's an extended family people do support each other, and you know if you're old then you don't have to worry because the younger generation always will look after you. But on the other hand some people ...

A ... I mean I suppose in this country people expect in many ways that the state is expected to take that role over, aren't they?

B Take the role exactly. (A: You know, that it's built into the family) Yes I suppose so and in that way it can be quite a lonely experience for older people. But the life in India can also be quite intrusive you know people can find that you know that ... (A: ... So it doesn't give much room for individuality) people know too much about their lives can can sort of force people to do things that they don't necessarily want to do ...

A ... And rather conservative as well I suppose, and fairly conservative as well I suppose in as much as people expect them to do things in the same way that they did.

2 Life in a kibbutz

- First brainstorm students on what a kibbutz is and what the lifestyle there is like. Students then read the facts and individually prioritise the various elements from the most positive (i.e. those which they most agree with) to the most negative. Encourage students to think about the rationale behind these ideas.

About 4% of Israel's population live in a kibbutz. The 'family' in a kibbutz has been shaped by a number of ideological and economic factors. Particularly during the early days, all able-bodied adults were needed to get the settlements off the ground which left little time for intimate relationships between mothers and children. There was a reaction against the traditional 'Jewish mamma', the supposedly overprotective Jewish mother, a well-known figure in American folklore and humour. Children are looked after collectively so that men and women are free to work on equal terms. However, recent years have seen an increase in the time parents spend with their offspring.

Family

1 Family ties

a

b

c

d

1 Why do we need families? Is the family ever likely to disappear as an institution?

2 Should the mother or the father be the head of the family (i.e. matriarchal and patriarchal)? What roles do the mother and father play in your society? And sons and daughters? Who is the boss in your family?

3 What influence have your parents had on your life? Whose influence was stronger – your mother's or your father's? Would you instil the values that your parents instilled in you into your children?

4 Is descent in your society patrilineal (i.e. all children take their father's surname), matrilineal (through the mother), or bilineal (through mother and father)? Should sons and daughters have equal inheritance rights?

5 Should members of a family all try to live in the same area?

6 What differences have you noted between family life in Britain/America/Australia etc., and family life in your own country?

2 Life in a kibbutz

1 Adults and children receive the goods and services they require from the kibbutz.

2 Everyone has the same things to share, therefore there is little jealousy.

3 Sexual equality is emphasised – there are no separate father and mother roles.

4 Adults eat in the communal dining room, food is cooked in the communal kitchen and services such as laundering are provided for the entire kibbutz rather than being the responsibility of the family.

5 Married couples share a single bedroom plus living room. They don't live with their children.

6 In some kibbutzim, children as young as four days old live away from their parents in an infant house; they then move on to a children's house etc.

7 Children sleep in communal dormitories where they are raised by child 'caretakers' and 'educators', who are allocated between six and eight children each.

8 The caretakers cannot look after all the children at the same time, so children have to help each other to do basic things such as washing, dressing, and learning to go to the bathroom.

9 Children usually see their parents for an hour or two each day, often visiting them in their apartment. These visits are viewed as 'fun time' rather than occasions for socialisation and child training.

3 Love and marriage

- Students read passage and discuss questions.

ⓘ 'Polygamy' is a generic word which covers both polygyny and polyandry; the latter is very rare, students may like to hypothesise why.

Listening

- Students listen and answer the questions about a Ugandan woman talking about polygamy in her country.
  Questions: **1** How many wives did her father and grandfather have? **2** What advantages does polygamy have?

1 *5 (father), 20 (grandfather)* **2** *replacement mothers*

Polygamy ah in Uganda is is accepted because it's part of the culture. My grandfather had 20 wives and ah they had a very very big compound and everybody lived together, each one of course, having his own house, and our own house. And ah my father had five wives and all of them, each one of them had their own hut and my father would visit them, would rotate once a week with each lady. And for us children it was a very beautiful place to grow up with because we had lots of er other children to play with. If a mother, suppose if a mother falls sick, or if she dies, or if she had to go some place, then automatically the other mothers would take care of the children of the one missing and for us children I think it was an ideal place to grow up in.

ⓘ Interestingly, this Ugandan lady who originally had a Ugandan husband, but is now married to an Italian, says that she has never thought of polygamy as being problematic and that the women don't think of it as being a bad thing at all. For those of you curious about the sexual part, she said that her father slept with his wives on a weekly basis – one week one wife, and then the next week another wife, etc. She also said that it was far better for men to be open about their sexual promiscuity (as it says in the text, the second wife is initially presented as a lover) than westerners who may do everything behind their partner's back.

4 Sacrifice?

- Students read the passage and answer the true/false statements. They then discuss their answers in groups. Then proceed to the listening.

Listening

- **NB** Make sure students have discussed question **e** on their pages before doing this exercise. Students hear a New Zealander, an American and an Indian (born in England) discussing what they will do with their parents when they get old.

Questions: **1** How old are the first speaker's parents? **2** Does he want to have his parents living with him – why? why not? **3** In India where do grandparents live? **4** Does the Indian woman want to have her parents living with her? Would they agree? **5** Why are old people's homes so 'terrible'? **6** What is the best solution?

1 *approaching 70s* **2** *no; unnatural* **3** *with their children* **4** *yes; maybe not* **5** *surrounded by only old people* **6** *granny flat*

A Well, I'm about that age where I have to decide what I'm going to do with my parents when they sort of reach an age when they're not going to be able to look after themselves. It's an interesting question, one that I haven't really thought about until now.

B How old are they now?

A They're er approaching seventies.

C Would you not have them living with you, do you think you would want that?

A Absolutely not.

B You wouldn't?

A Well, I'd rather not, no. I mean I know that sounds selfish but I really don't think I would like to have them living with me.

C That's interesting because in India, you know, of course a lot of the the grandparents live with their children and I mean they play a vital role in the home, you know what I mean, they're not just there ...

A ... But is that because they've always been in the home?

C They have, true.

A That's the difference because I think it would be such an unnatural situation to suddenly have them back or to be in a situation where they're there in sort of my world.

B Would you think of putting them in a home?

A Um, yeah, I suppose if that was the only alternative, yeah that would be what I'd do.

B And is that unthinkable as far as you're concerned?

C Well, it's interesting because my parents are so independent that in a sense I think they might think oh I'd rather go to a home. But really I, you know, I would feel happier if they if they came to me, but then because you know my partner isn't Indian, it's quite unusual, so I'd have to accommodate that within my home I think.

B I mean I'm just like Ralph, I'm a long way from my parents; the idea of them living with me does seem pretty weird and wild. But the terrible thing about homes, that I find, I have a couple of friends that I go and visit in homes, is that they're full of old people and I would think, if I were an old person, I would hate to be just surrounded by nothing but old people. I like some kind of cross section, I think that idea is sweeping them under the carpet.

A I think the best alternative, idea is what we call, is to have a 'granny flat', which is to have a house next door.

C Next door but separate enough to live in your own little space.

3 Love and marriage

About 25% of the world's people live in societies where husbands can have more than one wife. Before the age of industrialisation, this meant that a man could amass great wealth in acquiring several wives, although the wives themselves often maintained some kind of economic independence. The husband also played a relatively minor role in family life. However, in an age of compulsory education and increasingly equal rights for men and women, having extra wives and children has turned into an economic burden.

In many cases, when a man already has one or more wives, a potential 'new' wife is introduced into the family unit. Before she officially becomes a wife, she has to learn her future husband's ways, the food he likes etc. (!), and she also has to prove that she can fit in with the rest of the family. Then when the trial period is over, the marriage ceremony takes place.

1. What are the pros and cons of monogamy (one husband, one wife), polygyny (one husband, several wives), and polyandry (one wife, several husbands)?
2. Should parents be allowed to decide who their children marry? What are the advantages of an arranged marriage? What are the dangers of a marriage that is only based on personal compatibility?
3. Should marriages be to people outside the immediate circle of relatives or immediate community (exogamous), or restricted to one's own kin or social group (endogamous)? Is it better to marry someone from one's own social class and nationality?
4. What is the right age to get married?
5. Should couples be allowed to get divorced? If not, how should they resolve their problems? Why are divorce rates constantly increasing in the Western world, and what could be done to stop this increase?

4 Sacrifice?

Did Cindy and Roger Plum of Coon Rapids, Minnesota, overstep the limits of parental sacrifice to try to save their 9-year-old daughter Alyssa? Although their efforts failed, both parents say they would do it again – and again.

Last New Year's Eve, Alyssa took to bed with symptoms that suggested bronchitis. Three months later she was rushed to a hospital emergency room with a high fever. Doctors suspected a virus, but sent her home. Two days later, Alyssa was at her doctor's office with pneumonia. Within days her skin turned blue from lack of oxygen. By mid-April she was on a list for a lung transplant.

The Plums, who had read about transplant surgeries using lobes of the lung from living donors, decided to volunteer. Alyssa successfully received a piece of Roger's lung. Then her other lung failed. Less than four weeks later, Cindy underwent the procedure. This time Alyssa died of heart failure. Both parents have 45-cm scars that run from their chest to their back. Cindy's sleep is still interrupted by pain. Roger suffers from muscle weakness. Even though the couple have a son, Travis, 6, who risked losing a parent, they never had doubts about their actions. 'If I didn't give Alyssa a chance at life,' says Cindy, 'I didn't know if I could live with myself.' ■

a I would never do for my child what the Plums did.

b I don't see why parents have to put their child's interest before their own, e.g. going without some of the things they really want so that they can buy something for their child; or not playing their own sport so that they can watch their child playing his/her own sport.

c Children should not rely on their parents for money. They should try to do some holiday/Saturday jobs and become economically independent.

d Children should not be expected to do jobs around the house.

e Children have no responsibility towards their parents when they grow old. The children never asked to be born and parents should not expect their help.

Geography

Warm-ups

- Students draw quick outlines of five countries. They pass these to their partner, who has to write sentences like: I think this is France, this looks like Britain, this could be Australia, this must be Italy. They can then criticise each other's maps: this should have been bigger, you've missed out this part, etc.

1 Geography test

- Students answer questions **1–10** in groups and see which group can finish the test first. They can then check the answer in the key (statistics on questions **2** and **3** vary from source to source and year to year, so check with an up-to-date reference book). Students then discuss questions **11** and **12**.

Writing

- Students discuss one of the following: (a) If you could live anywhere in the world (apart from where you live now) where would it be? (b) Are people who live in cold climates greater achievers than those who live in warmer climates?

Listening

- Students hear some people discussing the effects of geographical location on people's lives and personality.
- Copy the table below on to the whiteboard, leaving out the answers. Students fill in the table while listening. 'Features' refers to geographical and natural features, and 'personality', to the effect that these features and climate have on the personality of the inhabitants.

(The tapescript for this exercise is on p. 36.)

⊶

	country	features	climate	personality
Speaker 1	*NZ*	*open space, beautiful nature, beaches, skiing*	*hot summers, cold winters*	*friendly, easy-going, relaxed*
Speaker 2	*USA*	*natural beauty, cities*		*east: reserved and hard; west: laid-back, warm, open*

Writing

- Students to choose two or three of the following and write about the implications of living under such conditions: in a remote mountain village, under a volcano, in a desert, in a third world country, in a desert, near a river which often floods, where there is no natural water supply, near a nuclear power station.

2 Settlements

- Brainstorm students on the life of primitive man. With a multinational class, you should get interesting input on the problems that man faced in different parts of the world. Focus the discussion in the following areas: food, shelter, defence, health, religion and death, industry and trade, entertainment.

ⓘ Life in Britain: In the Paleothic age (before 8000 BC) people lived by hunting, fishing and food gathering (e.g. nuts, roots and berries); often dwelled in caves; animals included bison, bear, rhino and hyena. Mesolithic (8000 – 3250 BC): no longer totally nomadic but still no permanent settlements; first evidence of temporary woodland clearances. Neolithic: began farming land with grain crops; settlements on high ground; burial chambers; extensive trade in stone axes. Bronze age (1700 – 500 BC): bronze weapons and ornamental objects; wood and stone still used for agricultural tools; more forest clearing; stone circles; evidence of lowland settlements. Iron age (500 BC–43 AD): hilltop forts serve as tribal capitals; farmsteads and small villages; cattle and sheep grazing; trade routes expanded.

- Give students the following instructions: Imagine that you are part of a primitive tribe. You have just moved to a new area and are deciding where to settle. Look at the map and decide on three alternative positions for your camp. Then decide on the best position.

Follow-up

- In a monolingual class, with a bit of imagination and some local maps, you could extend this exercise into modern times by getting students to think about possible locations for some of the following: a new town, disco, supermarket, sports centre, etc.
- Local geography: What do students know about the origins of the names of the places where they live? What do they know about local history.

ⓘ Some common English place names with Saxon and Norse origins: -bury/-borough etc. = fortified place; -bourne/-born = stream/spring; -ham = village/manor/homestead/enclosure; -leigh/-ley etc. = forest/wood/glade/clearing; -cester/-chester etc. from the Latin 'castra' meaning military base.

Geography

1 Geography test

1 Brazil, Canada, China, Russia, USA – put these in order of size.

2 Name three of the richest and three of the poorest countries in the world.

3 In which countries in the world are you likely to live longest?

4 Which is the longest river and the tallest mountain in the world?

5 How far is it from London to a) New York, b) Sydney?

6 What are the capitals of Australia, Egypt, India, Peru, Sweden?

7 What are the names of all the continents in order of size?

8 Which countries use the following currencies: dinar, drachma, franc, lira, yen?

9 In which countries do they not write from right to left: China, Iran, Iraq, India, Pakistan?

10 Can you recognise the following countries (some are mirror images, some upside-down)?

11 In your country, where are the worst and best places to live from a climate point of view?

12 Would you rather your country:
were smaller/bigger?
had hotter/colder summer/winters?
had more rain?
had fewer mountains?
had different neighbouring countries?
had a greater mix of nationalities?
had a different language(s)?

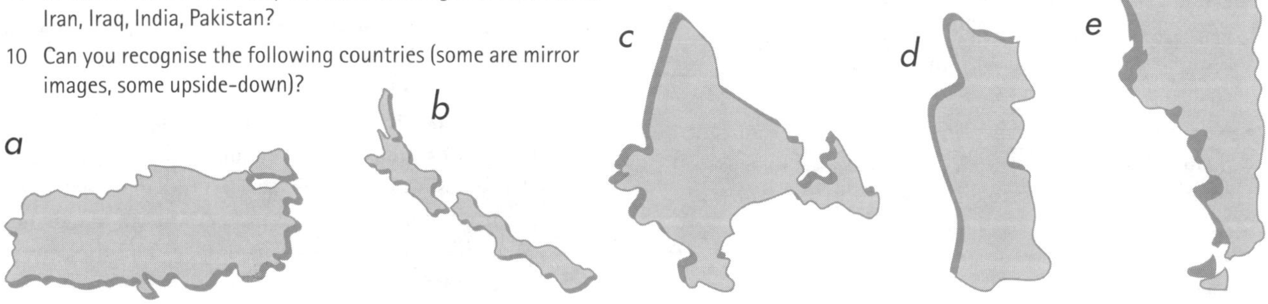

1 Russia (17m km²) Canada (9.7m km²) China (9.6m km²) USA (9.4m km²) Brazil (8.5m km²) **2** poor: Bangladesh, Bhutan, Burkina Faso, Malawi, Mozambique, Tanzania, Somalia; rich: Switzerland, Luxembourg, Japan **3** Japan, Iceland, Hong Kong **4** Nile; Everest (though some people say K2 is) **5** a) 5335km; b) 17005km **6** Canberra, Cairo, New Delhi, Lima, Stockholm **7** Asia (43m km²), Africa (30m²), North and Central America (25m²), South America (17m²), Antarctica (13m²), Europe (10m²), Australasia (9m²) **8** dinar: Algeria, Bahrain, Iraq, Jordan, Kuwait, Libya, Tunisia, the countries of the former Yugoslavia; drachma: Greece; franc: Belgium, France (and ex-Belgian and ex-French colonies) Liechtenstein, Luxembourg, Switzerland; lira: Italy, Malta, Turkey; yen: Japan **9** China, India **10** a Turkey b New Zealand c India d Portugal e Argentina

2 Settlements

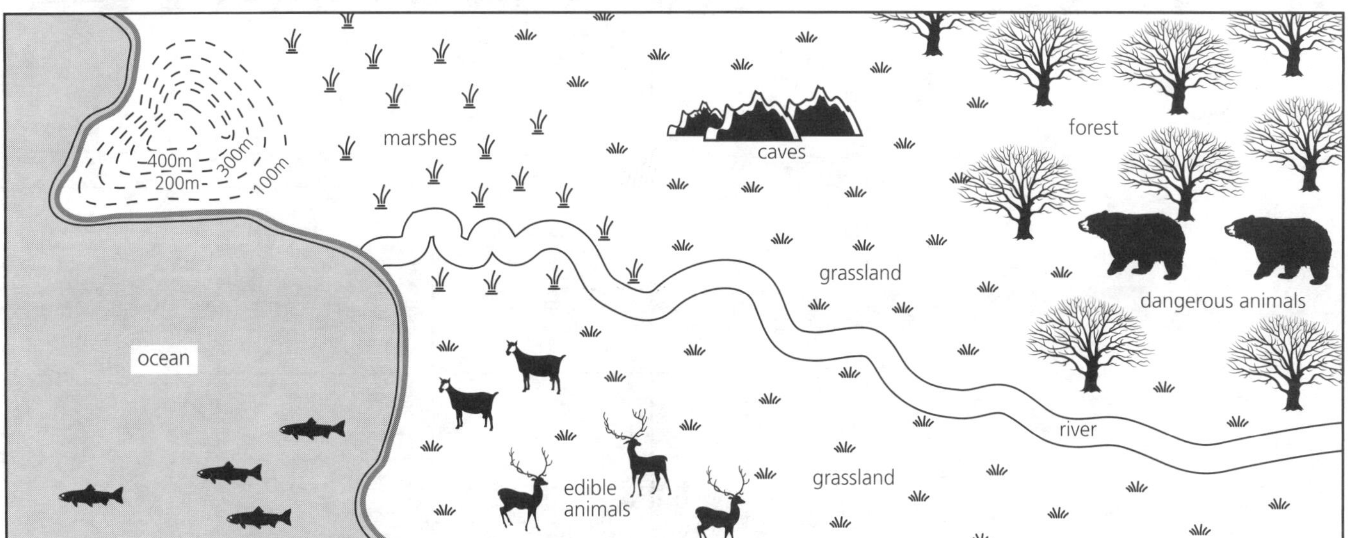

Geography

3 The Peters Projection

I used the *Peters Atlas of the World* (Longman) for this exercise. I would thoroughly recommend buying this atlas, as it has some really fascinating thematic maps on such things as languages, religions, education, child labour, inequality, status of women etc., which I have used very productively with my students.

- Ask students to cover the Peters Projection and focus their attention on the traditional map (the top one) . Get them to compare the relative sizes of Greenland (2,175,600 km²) and Australia (7,682,300 km²), to estimate which is the bigger and how much bigger it is (Australia is more than three times as big). Elicit the main problem of map-making (i.e. how to represent a three dimensional globe on a two-dimensional map). Explain that Mercator, the Flemish cartographer, whose map, published in 1569, is the basis of our modern maps, resolved the problem by treating the world as a cylinder (north up, south down) to make life easy for navigators.
- Now get students to look at the Peters Projection, and ask them now about the relative proportion of the various countries. Get students to think about why such a map was made, and how it affects our world view.

ⓘ Mercator placed Europe in the centre of his world picture. And since the southern hemisphere was something of an irrelevance in 1569, he relegated it to the bottom third of the map. Peters drew the earth in 'equal-area' and in the atlas itself, all pages are of equal scale and representation. This also means third world countries become much more prominent on the map.

- Finally, ask students to read the two passages and decide which comes from the introduction to the Peters Atlas and which from a review.

Key: **1** *Intro* **2** *Review (The Economist)*

Follow-up

- This exercise involves students rearranging the relative positions of countries in the world and then talking about what the effects would be.
- Photocopy the map below (increasing it in size, photocopier permitting. **NB** the position of Australia has been slightly lowered to make it all fit on to one card). You will need one copy for each group of students. Paste the map on to a piece of cardboard. Cut the map up into twelve parts as indicated. On the back of each resulting card put an upward arrow to indicate which way the card should be placed (otherwise some countries might appear upside-down).
- Give each group a set of cards face down. Tell them to arrange the cards, with the arrows pointing upwards, to make a four (width) by three (height) rectangle. Now instruct them to turn over the cards from left to right, i.e. picking up a card from the left hand side and, and turning it over so that the left side becomes the right side (you can show them how this should be done). They should now have a rearranged map of the world.
- Now tell them to imagine that this is a new world, though the equators and climatic conditions remain in the same relative positions as before, i.e. countries in the extreme north and south are cold, countries in the middle are hot. In groups ask them to discuss what implications these new positions would have.
- They should think in terms of: climate (how this would affect the people, agriculture and economy); politics (new political or military alliances may be necessary); resources (countries may now have access to resources that they didn't have before, e.g. to oil from neighbouring countries or water; they may have a port that they didn't have before, or their country may even have been chopped in half and the two halves are in different parts of the world!).
- Finally, get students to walk from group to group and then decide whose 'new world order' is the best.

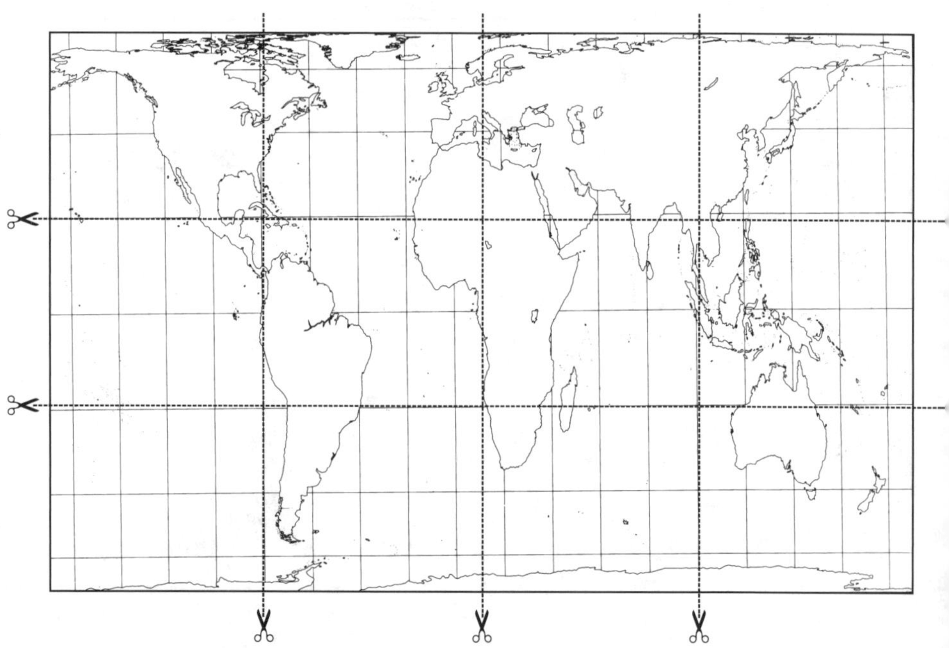

3 The Peters Projection

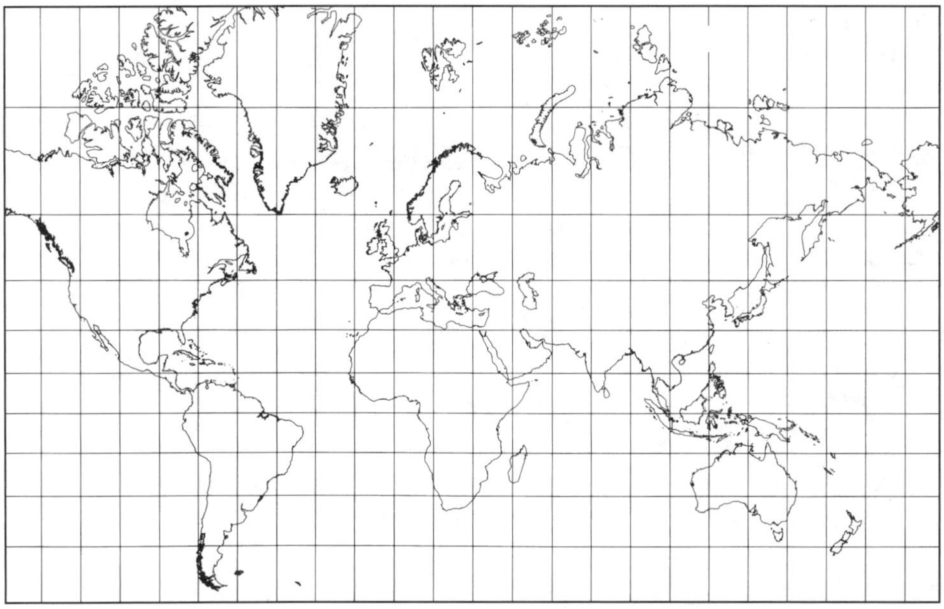

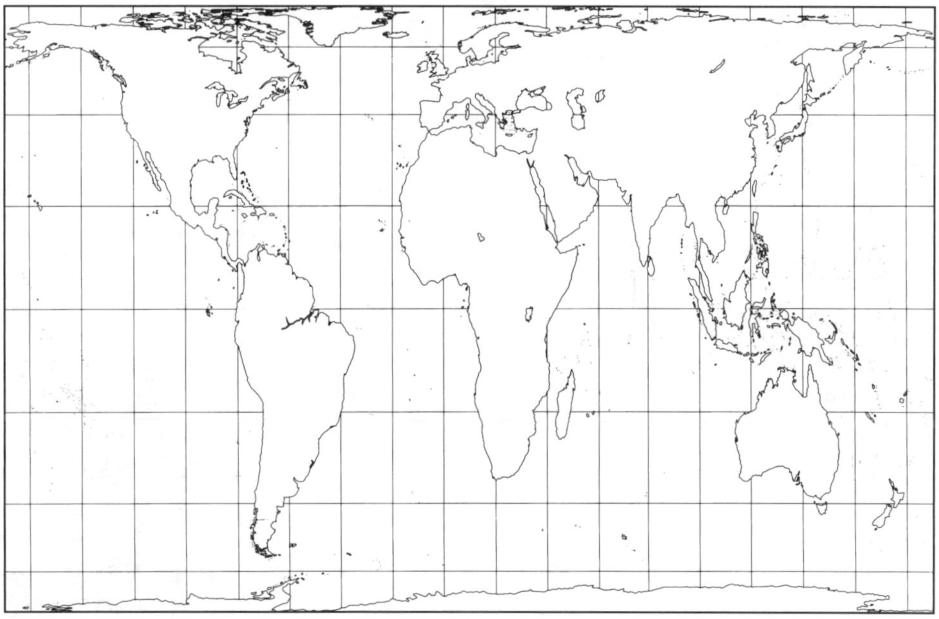

1

We have come to accept as 'natural' a representation of the world that devotes disproportionate space to large-scale maps of areas perceived as important, while consigning other areas to small-scale general maps. And it is because our image of the world has become thus conditioned, that we have for so long failed to recognise the distortion for what it is – the equivalent of peering at Europe and North America through a magnifying glass and then surveying the rest of the world through the wrong end of a telescope. There is nothing 'natural' about such a view of the world. It is the remnant of colonialism and fired by that age.

2

In the Peters Projection, Chad and Nigeria both keep their proper areas, but are shown twice as long north-south as they really are. His oddly bottom-heavy, etiolated world picture (one in which the third world is visually prominent) is dismissed by rivals as a piece of cartographic plagiarism. According to one critic, it looks as though Mr Peters hung the continents from the Arctic Circle while they were still wet. By contrast, international aid organisations – especially UNICEF – have embraced the Peters map as the only true representation of the world, and have championed its cause by distributing 60 million copies.

Honesty

Warm-up

- Brainstorm students on what they prefer in a person: honesty/sincerity, intelligence, sense of humour, good looks. They should put the four in order of priority. If they all come up with the same order, get them to justify the inverse order, i.e. if they have put good looks as being the least important, they should think of justifications for it being the most important.

1 How honest are you?

- Before giving students any photocopies, put students in groups and get them to make up their own test/quiz in any format they like for deciding how honest their companions are. A final version in written form can then be photocopied and distributed as a reading and discussion exercise for the next lesson.
- Alternatively, students go directly to the quiz on their page. They should first answer the questions individually and then discuss them in pairs.

Writing

- Given the opportunity most people would steal if there was no way of being caught. Discuss.

2 White lies

- Ask students to discuss in groups how they can tell if someone is lying, whether lying is actually bad, who we lie most often to and what it is that we lie about. Then get feedback from whole class.

ⓘ Whilst we are all very good at telling lies we are not so good as spotting them. Unless someone is a professional/complusive liar there are a number of things that people tend to do when they lie: they tend to avoid eye-contact; their voice has a higher pitch than usual; what they say sounds rehearsed – probably using words that are supposed to be convincing but generally sound unnatural and distant; they tend to touch their nose or ears, scratch parts of their body, and shift in their seat. Interestingly, we tend to lie more to attractive people rather than unattractive people. Most lies are not intended to be deceptive; generally we lie unconsciously, either to be tactful or to protect/promote ourselves, by editing out details. Lying is not always a bad thing; married couples who religiously tell each other everything are more likely to get divorced than those who have a few secrets. In any case, imagine what life would be like if we always told the truth!

- In groups, students discuss in which of the situations it would be convenient to tell a white lie. They say what the lie might be and whether they would actually use it.

Tapescript for **Geography 1 Geography test**

A Well, I grew up in New Zealand so I suppose I had the advantage of being in a place where there was so much open space and beautiful nature that anything seemed possible and very easy to, to, to, everything was easy to do, the beaches were only ten minutes away, the skiing was sort of only an hour away, so it was a really easy sort of way of living.

B Are the people friendlier as a consequence, do you think?

A I think they're more easy-going. I think, just because everything was accessible people have a slightly more relaxed way of life.

B Is it hot, New Zealand? I don't know much about its climate.

A The climate's quite extreme I suppose, summers are hot and the winters are cold. The winters are similar to the British winters.

B I mean I also come from a large country of outstanding natural beauty, but, it's got lots of big cities as well. America has many different countries and consequently there are many different kinds of people who live there. In the east they're more reserved and harder, in the west they're more laid-back, warmer, more open. Em I live in England now and it's quite different, they're an island people aren't they? But I find it suits me because California, where I'm from, I was considered to be very reserved in personality – believe it or not – whereas here I'm considered quite open, simply by contrast.

Honesty

1 How honest are you?

Rate the following for dishonesty

(1: perfectly OK 5: totally dishonest)

		1	2	3	4	5
1	Using public transport without buying a ticket.	☐	☐	☐	☐	☐
2	Getting someone else to do your homework for you.	☐	☐	☐	☐	☐
3	Making an event sound much better or worse than it really was.	☐	☐	☐	☐	☐
4	Borrowing things without the owner's permission.	☐	☐	☐	☐	☐
5	Promising to visit / phone / write to someone when you have no intention of doing so.	☐	☐	☐	☐	☐
6	Not telling the waiter/waitress that they've undercharged you for your meal.	☐	☐	☐	☐	☐
7	Telling your children that Father Christmas exists.	☐	☐	☐	☐	☐
8	Copying books, CDs, videos and computer software.	☐	☐	☐	☐	☐
9	Cheating on your partner.	☐	☐	☐	☐	☐
10	Reading other people's diaries and letters without their permission.	☐	☐	☐	☐	☐

2 White lies

1 Your mother knits you a revolting jumper for your birthday.

2 A new friend invites you for dinner. You're doing nothing but you don't want to go.

3 You are a doctor. Your patient has six months to live.

4 Your child is 13. To get reduced rail fares she should be under 13.

5 Your partner has been hours preparing to go out for dinner. He/She looks terrible.

3 Cheating

- Tell students to cover the text. Students answer the true and false questions, then discuss them in their groups.
- Read or dictate the text. Students check what they've heard or had dictated against the printed text and correct the true and false answers where necessary.
- Brainstorm students on ways that adults cheat (e.g. tax dodges, drugs for sports performance enhancement, politicians, infidelity, lying to their kids).

Thanks to David Barnes for his suggestions throughout this unit and the next unit.

4 Hippocratic Oath

Some fairly heavy discussion might come out of this exercise.

- Get students to cover the text and questions. Brainstorm them on what the Hippocratic Oath is and what kind of promises they imagine that doctors have to make. Then get them to read the text and to discuss the reasons behind the oaths and the consequent implications. **NB** Nowadays virtually no doctors take the oath.

Implications: **3** *This could initiate a discussion on Jehovah's witnesses.* **4** *euthanasia* **5** *abortion*

Before the Declaration of Geneva in 1948, the Hippocratic Oath used to read as follows:

I will prescribe regimen for the good of my patients and never do harm to anyone. To please no one will I prescribe a deadly drug, nor give advice which may cause his death. Into whatever house I enter I will go into it for the benefit of the sick, and will abstain from every voluntary act of mischief and corruption. Whatever in connection with my professional practice or not in connection with it, I see or hear in the lives of men which ought not to be spoken of abroad, I will not divulge, as reckoning that all such should be kept secret. While I continue to keep this oath inviolate, may it be granted me to enjoy life and the practice of the art, respected by all men in all times, but should I trespass and violate this oath, may the reverse be my lot.

Writing

- Promises are made to be broken. Discuss.

3 Cheating

True or False?

You never cheated at school.

About 20% of children cheat at school.

More boys cheat than girls.

It is wrong to report on a cheat.

Have you ever copied someone else's answers in an exam or passed off someone else's term paper as your own original work? Sadly enough, if your reply is 'no', you are in a minority. Surveys have shown that about two thirds of children admitted cheating in school. Cheating is done more by males than females, and intelligence is unrelated (though those with below average grades cheat more than those with above average grades).

When you allow others to cheat without reporting their behaviour, your response is no different than the situation in which you stand idly by as a thief gets away with his or her crime. You may one day find yourself driving across a bridge designed by an individual who cheated on his engineering school exams, or you have a cavity filled by a dentist who was only able to pass dental school by copying the answers of a friend.

4 Hippocratic Oath

HIPPOCRATES WAS THE FOUNDER OF MODERN MEDICINE. HE WAS BORN ON THE ISLAND OF COS AROUND 460 BC, AND IS REGARDED AS THE MOST PROGRESSIVE PHYSICIAN OF ANCIENT TIMES. HE CREATED A CLEAR DISTINCTION BETWEEN WITCHCRAFT, RELIGION AND MEDICINE, AND A VERSION OF THE HIPPOCRATIC OATH DECLARED IN GENEVA IN 1948 IS BASED ON HIPPOCRATES' IDEAS.

Below are some of the promises that doctors have to make before entering their profession.

1 The health of my patient will be my first consideration.

2 I will not disclose any information that I see or hear in the lives of my patients. I will respect the secrets which are confided in me, even after the patient has died.

3 I will not permit consideration of religion, nationality, race, party politics or social standing to intervene between my duty and my patient.

4 I will not prescribe any deadly drug, nor give any advice that may cause my patient's death.

5 I will maintain the utmost respect for human life from the time of conception; even under threat, I will not use my medical knowledge contrary to the laws of humanity.

Ideas

Warm-up

- Get students to think of novel uses for three of the six things illustrated (TV remote control, zip, magnet, tennis racket, human being, rubber). They should try to extend their ideas beyond obvious uses: the remote control could obviously be used for switching other things off and on (including people we don't want to hear); the rubber could be used to cancel bad memories; an Austrian surgeon once sewed a zip into a man's stomach so that it was instantly accessible for internal dressings.

ⓘ Many books have been written containing exercises in which children or adults think of novel uses for everyday things (the most commonly used item for this exercise is probably a brick, others have been a paper clip, barrel, blanket, bucket, ladder, shoe). They are designed to test divergent and convergent thinkers. Convergent tests are typically IQ tests where there is only one possible answer; divergent tests require the examinee to think in an open-ended fashion, without examining one particular line of reasoning in detail. Scientists tend to be associated with convergent thinking, and artists with divergent thinking.

Listening

- Students hear about the origins of jeans. First brainstorm them with the following questions: **1** Why are jeans called jeans? **2** What is the name of the material used? **3** Where does this name come from? **4** Who invented jeans? **5** Who for? **6** What nationality was the inventor?
- Now get students to do the listening, and check their answers to the questions.

1 *After Strauss' wife Jean or may have derived from Genoa.* **2** *denim* **3** *serge de Nîmes cloth* **4** *Levi Strauss* **5** *lumberjacks etc.* **6** *German*

Levi Strauss was a poor young German immigrant who landed in New York in the 1840s in search of fortune. In 1850 he found himself caught up in the great Gold Rush in California. He had been informed in New York that canvas would fetch a good price from the gold miners, who needed it for tents and wagon covers. But on arrival in San Francisco, he met a miner who told them that he should have brought trousers instead, because none of the available ones could withstand the wear and tear down the mines. So Levi decided to use the canvas to make trousers instead. He soon gave up the idea of gold-digging and before long he had a thriving shop. The cloth he used was called 'serge de Nîmes', which the American salesmen quickly shortened to 'denims'.

'Levis' as they became known, were worn by prospectors, cowboys, farmers, lumberjacks, railroad construction men, oil drillers, and town people who wanted hard-wearing trousers. They were also known as 'blue jeans', and legend says that this name came about because Levi's wife, Jean, took a hand in shaping and sewing the trousers in the early days of the business. Another origin of the word 'jeans' is from the Italian town of Genoa, where the fabric for producing jeans was supposedly originally made.

1 Fixed ideas?

Consider the religious views of your students carefully before deciding to use this exercise.

- Brainstorm students on in what sense ideas can be considered as 'fixed'. Get them to think of some of their parents' and grandparents' fixed ideas, move the subject on to traditions and religious ideas. If suitable, compare fixed ideas in Britain (or wherever) and students' own countries.
- Pre-teach some legal vocabulary from the text. Students now read the text and answer true or false to the statements. Before they discuss their answers do the listening exercise (see below). In like-minded groups, ask them to think why other religions think in such a different way, and what problems this causes to world peace, harmony and understanding (wow!).

ⓘ The evolution controversy is still alive today. Various groups, including the Creationists (an offshoot of the Fundamentalists), actively campaign for the mandatory teaching of the Bible in schools in America. Incidentally, Darwin had a degree in theology.

Listening

- Students hear someone's views on this matter. This is designed to provoke some of the more narrow-minded (at least in my opinion). Students' task is to understand which questions **1–5** the speaker discusses and what he thinks about them.

1 *no, because he was teaching established scientific fact* **2** *parents have rights, for example whether their child should be taught religion or not.*

1 I think that in this case rather than the the science teacher being prosecuted I think the Fundamentalists should have been prosecuted. I think religious groups have no right at all to decide what can be taught in schools, and certainly not to tell teachers not to teach what is in fact established scientific evidence.

2 I do think that parents have a right to decide what their children are taught in schools. Personally, I don't want my child to be taught religion. I'd better amplify a little on that. I'm happy for my child to be to be taught religion but the religions of the world not just one particular religion. He lives in a Catholic country and I don't see why he should only hear the Catholic point of view.

Writing

- 'There is only one truth.' Discuss.

Ideas

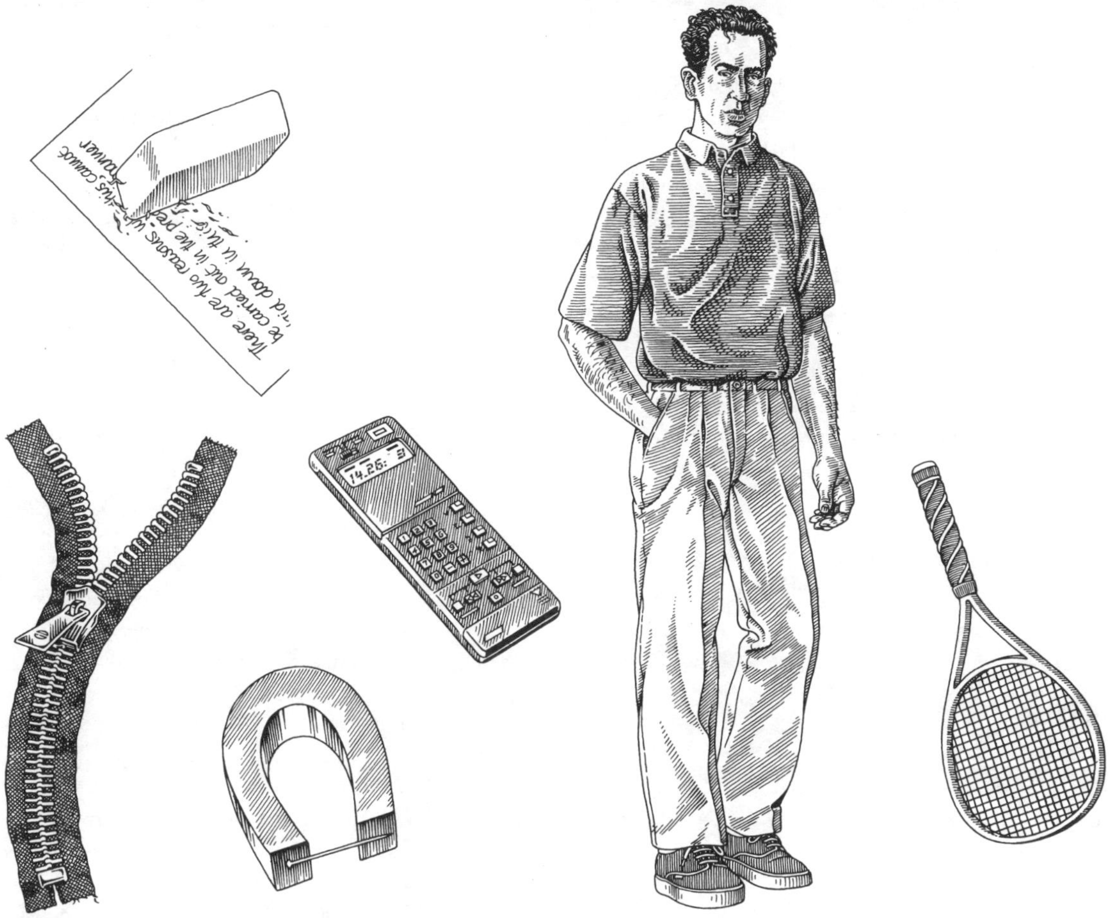

1 Fixed ideas?

In 1925, an American science teacher, J. T. Scopes, was prosecuted for teaching Darwin's theory of evolution in a school in Tennessee. Scopes was found guilty. However, when the case went to appeal, he managed to avoid conviction on a technicality. Scopes had been brought to court by a group of Presbyterian Fundamentalists, whose church had considerable power in the state of Tennessee.

Fundamentalism is the name given to a Protestant religious movement in America founded at the beginning of the twentieth century. One of the basic 'Fundamentals' is that the Bible (both Old and New Testaments) is totally accurate and should therefore be interpreted literally. This is in direct contradiction with Darwin's teachings on creation, which state that man originated from the apes. This thesis subsequently became accepted scientific fact.

Fundamentalists also believe that the Second Coming of Jesus Christ is imminent; that Mary, Christ's mother, was a virgin; and that the dead will be physically resurrected. Many also believe in the existence of eternal hell.

Over the years this has led to anti-Communist activities, and campaigns against abortion, homosexuality, pornography and equal rights. Most Fundamentalists do not smoke or drink alcohol, and generally don't dance, or go to the cinema and theatre.

1 No one has the right to convict a teacher for teaching what they believe is scientific evidence, or indeed any other belief they have.

2 Parents should have no say in what their children are taught in schools.

3 Sacred texts are 100% accurate and should be interpreted literally.

4 Religious authorities have a duty to impose certain sexual restrictions on their members.

5 It is immoral to smoke, drink alcohol, dance, and go to the cinema and theatre.

2 Any ideas?

- In this exercise students have to draw a design for one or more of the machines. In groups, they should first decide which machines it would actually be feasible to create. When the 'impossible' machines have been eliminated, still in their groups students should then narrow their choice down to four. Each individual now makes a drawing of one of these four machines, but without specifying which, nor writing any explanations. They then show each other their drawings and have to guess what they are supposed to depict. They then explain how their machine works while the others make criticisms. You may wish to set the drawing part for homework, and then discuss the machines in the next lesson.

Writing

- Students write to the patents office putting forth their idea for one of the machines and explaining why it is so good.

3 Strange ideas?

- Students read the 'thinking' text. Brainstorm suggestions as to who the Papalagi might be. Give students the information below.

ⓘ Tuiavii, a wise man of a tribe from Samoa, travelled to Europe in the early 1900s, and came into contact with the habits of the 'Papalagi' – the white men. On his return to his native islands, he warned his people against the perverse attraction of Western life. Erich Scheurmann, an artist friend of Hermann Hesse, who was in Samoa to escape the horrors of the First World War, made a collection of Tuiavii's criticisms of the mistaken values of the Europeans, in a book. What we read there makes us question the whole quality of our lives, through the eyes of someone totally unaffected by the so-called progress of mankind. Scheurmann divided Tuiavii's insights into different sections, some of which are summarised on the student's pages. These passages are my very free translations of an Italian translation (*Stampa Alternativa*) of a German book.

- Before reading the two other extracts, ask students what they think a native of the tribe might say about 'things' and 'time' in the context of Western culture.
- Now, students read the passages and then discuss the ideas in them. Alternatively each student chooses one passage to read and then explains the ideas to someone who has read a different passage.

Writing

- Students imagine what Tuiavii might have said about newspapers and money. Imaginative students might even be able to write in Tuiavii's style.

2 Any ideas?

1 A means of learning more but studying less.

2 A machine to torture bad teachers.

3 A car for specific people: a painter, a rock musician, a man of religion, a prostitute.

4 A device for automatically doing your homework.

5 The school of the future.

6 A language machine.

7 A machine to convert silence into gold.

8 A house specially designed for blind people.

9 A method of irrigation for desert areas.

10 A machine for making dreams come true.

3 Strange ideas?

THINKING

A Papalagi thinks the whole time, so much so that his head is the only part of his body that he uses. When the sun shines, he immediately thinks: 'How magnificently the sun is shining.' This is wrong, absolutely wrong, because when the sun shines it's much better not to think of anything at all. A wise Samoan just lies there under the sun and thinks of nothing, and lets his whole body soak in the sun, so that each part of his body becomes happy. When a white man sees a mountain he thinks 'I wonder what's on the other side', instead of admiring how beautiful the mountain is in itself. He thinks about what will happen to him when he dies, instead of living now.

THINGS

If all the men in a Samoan village put all their things together, they wouldn't have as many things as the Papalagi have in one house. Some have so many things that they have to employ other people to spend their day tidying and dusting these things. There are men who kill themselves because they prefer to die rather than live without things. If they came to live in a Samoan hut, they wouldn't know what to do, they'd have to go into the forest and find things to fill the hut up. Their hands never stop moving – they have to be continually making things, and then making more things to put those things in, boxes inside boxes, inside boxes. I heard a Papalagi talking about our island: 'We've got to create needs for them.' And by needs he meant things. We've got to be on guard against the Papalagi, his words may seem like sweet bananas, but they're really poisoned arrows.

When a man says: 'This is my head and it doesn't belong to anyone else but me', we would all agree. But he also says 'This palm tree is mine' just because it happens to grow in front of his house. But the palm isn't his and never will be. It's God's. In our language we use the word 'lau' which means both mine and yours. For the Papalagi there is nothing more distinct than mine and yours. If you dare to touch one of his things outside his house he will call you a thief, and you will be tied up in chains. And think, even if a Papalagi has enough mats for a hundred people to sleep on, and food enough to fill his whole house, he doesn't go out and try to help people who have nowhere to sleep or nothing to eat.

TIME

The Papalagi never has enough time. He has even divided the day up, like we cut up a coconut. And all the parts have a name: seconds, minutes, hours. I've never been able to understand this system, and anyway there's no point thinking about such infantile things. When one of their time machines sounds, he says: 'Oh no, an hour has already gone by.' I don't really understand this obsession, I think it's a serious illness. There are Papalagi who say they never have time, and they run around as if they were possessed by the devil. They don't realise that the time is there if they want it. They even count how many moons there have been seen since someone was born, and they make great sacrifices with flowers and banquets, when someone has lived a certain number of moons. Many thought 'I should be ashamed of myself when I didn't know how old I was.' And I just thought to myself, 'It's much better not to know.' The Papalagi spends his whole time devising ways of having more time: he puts wheels under his feet, gives wings to his words. But in the end what does he do with his time?

Jobs

Warm-up

- Dictate this list: Write down two jobs which:
  1 can be done by robots
  2 no longer exist
  3 require absolutely no intelligence
  4 have low salaries but high prestige
  5 require very long training
  6 will be most needed in the future
  7 are overpaid
  8 young children typically want to do
  9 can be done from home
  10 you would really hate to do
- In five minutes students have to try and write down two jobs which correspond to the categories. Make this activity competitive by seeing which person or group manages to finish the task first. Students then discuss and dispute their answers.
- Alternatively, or if students are having problems coming up with ideas, put them in pairs, and then put pairs into groups until they complete the list.

1 What is work?

- Students read the quotation by Andy Warhol, the American pop artist, and then brainstorm them on their concept of 'work'. Then get students to discuss questions **2**, **3** and **4** in groups.

Writing

- Students choose one of these titles: (a) My ideal job. (b) A day in the life of a ... (c) How I would resolve unemployment.

2 Which job?

Listening

- Students discuss **1** and **2** only. Do the first part of the listening (i.e. as far as ** '... for me that would be the most boring job'). Students compare their opinions with the speakers. Listen again to focus on the language used and pick out some expressions (e.g. overall, what about, would have to be). Students now complete the activity trying to use some of the expressions used by the native speakers. Now play the last part of the listening. Once again students should note down the choice of job and the reasons given for this.

1 *baby-sitter (likes kids anyway, not hard work)* **2** *assembly line worker (repetitive)* **3** *doctor (time never your own, horrible hours)* **4** *(not mentioned)* **5** *soldier (might have to kill someone)*

A What do you think is the easiest job?

B Em I think probably the baby-sitter, I mean I know there is a responsibility obviously of looking after somebody else's baby, but I think overall em probably you'd like children anyway, so you would actually enjoy doing the job. Yeah and it wouldn't really be hard work. For me that would certainly be the easiest. Um what about the second one, erm what do you think would be the most boring job?

A I think the most boring job would have to be an assembly line worker because you're looking and doing, you're looking at the same things over and over day after day doing the same task over and over day after day. And your day is broken up into periods that are always the same, same time for break, lunch, etc., so definitely that would be for me the most boring job.** But the most tiring job ...

B That's a difficult one, they're all tiring but in different ways actually, but I think probably being a doctor because it seems really that your time is never your own if you're in a general practice anyway; actually even in hospitals of course they work terrible hours.

A Um what about the worst job?

B The worst job? I think well, it would have to be a soldier simply because erm you might end up having to kill someone.

Jobs

1 What is work?

'I suppose I have a really loose interpretation of 'work', because I think that just being alive is so much work at something you don't always want to do.' (Andy Warhol)

1 Apart from school or your job, what else do you consider to be work?

2 Are these 'real' jobs: housewife, monarch, novelist, pop star, priest?

3 If the salary were the same, which job would you like to do: actor/actress, archaeologist, astronomer, chef, fashion designer, fortune teller, musician, research scientist, tourist operator?

4 If you had enough money never to have to work again, would you stop working? What would you do instead?

2 Which job?

1 Which is the easiest job?
baby-sitter, dentist, footballer, teacher

2 The most boring?
car park attendant, assembly line worker, shepherd, window cleaner

3 The most tiring?
doctor, farmer, miner, top model

4 The most useful?
journalist, market researcher, nurse, postman/woman

5 The worst?
grave digger, prison warder, soldier, toilet cleaner

3 Dirty jobs?

- Ask students to cover question 7.
- Students make their decisions individually, and then discuss in groups. Students should then reformulate their decisions on the basis of the follow-up question 7.

Writing

- (a) Write a letter to the managing director of one of these companies, trying to convince him/her to change the company policy. (b) Write a press release from one of these companies which wants to set up in your area. The statement should justify why, for example, testing beauty products on animals is needed and is not immoral.

4 Industrial tribunal

ⓘ An industrial tribunal is a court of justice, whose job is to deal with cases related to work. They have a legally qualified chairperson and two lay members who have knowledge or experience of employment in industry or commerce.

- Ask students to read all four situations without discussing them. Tell students that the four people believe they have been unfairly dismissed by their employer. Students then imagine that they are members of a (3/4 person) jury whose job is to decide: (a) what the real motivations for the dismissals were (b) whether they really have been unfairly dismissed and (c) if so what kind of compensation should be given to them.

Listening

- Students hear two people arguing about one of the industrial tribunal cases. Their task is simply to identify which case is being talked about, and whether the two speakers agree that the person was unfairly dismissed.
- Play the tape again and pick out some relevant phrases, which you would like students to use in their own discussions. Students now decide which of the two people in the listening they agree with and proceed to discuss the other three cases.

case **3** *(the captain): The woman thinks he should have been dismissed, the man doesn't.*

A And I think that it's an absolutely awful thing to have done, because he's he's he's the guy in charge, he's the one that history dictates he has to stay there, I'm sure his job description dictates that he does as well, and he's cleared off, leaving the hundred and sixty, whether or not he was hoping that they'd die or not I'm not sure. I'm in absolute agreement that he was dismissed for unethical behaviour and I agree with it.

B No, I think that's absolute nonsense I'm afraid, I'm sorry. I mean why? You know, there's a saying the captain has to go down with his ship, well why? I mean why on earth should the captain die?

A Because he's the man in charge.

B Yeah, but so what? So that means he's in a position to be able to leave the ship, which is absolutely right, quite right, I would have done exactly the same thing.

ⓘ **1**, **3** and **4** are based on real situations, but **1** and **3** were not actually taken to an industrial tribunal; **4** lost his case on the grounds that he was fully aware of what he was doing when he signed the contract. In America, where some companies pay for their employees' ever-increasing health insurance costs, some employers think they should be able to dictate what their workers do both at work and at home. This ranges from discouraging workers not to have high calorie diets to prohibiting workers from smoking at home, and stopping their managers from using motorbikes. Are these kinds of impositions acceptable? If students were employers, are there certain categories of people who they would not want to give a job to, or who they would be prepared to dismiss if they infringed some of their 'regulations'?

Writing

- Students choose one of the four people and write a letter of complaint to their ex-boss. Students should try and justify what they did and why they should be reinstated.

5 Honesty at work

- Get students to rank the situations in terms of how dishonest they are. Students then discuss their ranking in pairs.

3 Dirty jobs?

Which of these organisations would you work for if you had little or no alternative?

1 A pharmaceutical company which tests its beauty products on animals.

2 A multinational which trades with the governments of politically oppressed people.

3 An arms producer or a company whose products can be used for military purposes.

4 A fast food chain that opens 'restaurants' in beautiful squares in the old quarters of towns.

5 A nuclear power station.

6 A tobacco company.

7 How honest were you in answering these questions? If you had no other opportunities for getting a job, is there no way you would reconsider? How much is one really contributing to the problem by working for such companies?

4 Industrial tribunal

1 This German presenter hosted a TV show which assembled groups of journalists to discuss topical problems. At its height, and as a result of the ability of the presenter, the programme attracted 100 million viewers. He lost his job after revelations that he was a 'desk war criminal'; during the Second World War he had written newspaper articles in favour of Nazi activities, such as executions.

2 This air hostess was sacked after she returned rather overweight to work, six months after giving birth. The airline company claimed that their image would suffer and that the hostess was having difficulty moving down the aisle in the plane.

3 This captain was the first to leave his sinking ship. He escaped on a helicopter where he claimed he was able to co-ordinate the operation better. He left 160 passengers on board, all of whom survived. He was dismissed for unethical behaviour.

4 This man, whose job involved high precision technical work, was dismissed for drinking alcohol at home on a Sunday night. He had signed a contract which stated that he was not allowed to smoke, drink alcohol or take high-cholesterol snacks either at work or home.

5 Honesty at work

How wrong
do you think the following activities are?

1 Inadvertently cancelling information on a computer and failing to report the fact.

2 A woman at a job interview who doesn't say that she is two months' pregnant.

3 Phoning up to say you're ill, when you're not, to get a day (or days) off.

4 Making personal photocopies on the company's photocopier.

5 Lying about your qualifications at a job interview.

6 Drinking a lot of alcohol during the work break.

7 Stealing office supplies (e.g. pens and paper).

8 Taking longer breaks than are authorised.

9 Cheating on the expense account.

10 Selling company secrets.

Kindness

Warm-ups

- Ask students if they have ever given or would give any of the following to an unknown person: their blood, parts of their body, their sperm, their time, their money.

- How much money would students spend on: a wedding present for a close friend, a leaving present for a teacher, mother's birthday present, sister/brother's Christmas (or equivalent) present? The right amount of money will vary considerably from country to country.

1 Love thy neighbour

- Students read the text and answer question **1** as whole class activity. Ask students what they would have done in such situations. Then do the listening.

Listening

- Students hear some native speakers discussing the two situations. Students have to decide which explanations in question **2 a–f** are mentioned, and if the speakers believe they are true or false.

a *T* **b** *T* **c** *T* **d** *not mentioned, but this is confirmed by the football example (the player in question was Cantona)* **e** *don't know, but probably not* **f** *T*

A I'm afraid I'm of the school that thinks that basically people are out for themselves and are rather cowardly. And I think in both cases that's proved by this story, I think you know, these stories, I mean first of all people, if you hear someone screaming in the middle of the night, and you think that sounds dangerous, you do nothing, you think I'm not going anywhere near that, so you want to protect yourself and that explains why people stand back and watch someone get killed in front of them. And and as for the man finding the money in the bottom of the box and giving it back, I think that's also fear, that's a fear of being caught.

B ... being caught. Yes, I think I tend to agree with that actually.

C But I thought that was in that situation there was no chance that he could get caught.

A But ... but, but it's not a rational thing, is it? You know. I mean (Oh that someone, somewhere), that someone, somewhere, that in fact they've done it to trap you.

C So there's no such thing as a noble motive in your opinion?

A I don't know. I think that people can, but then that may well be a sort of self promotional thing.

C I have an idea of why it might might happen, and that is that we're originally tribal, not individuals, and we've lost that, and we've become more and more and more individual, so there's nothing really to take care of that, but the yearning for it is shown in things like Live Aid, Mother Teresa, charities and so on. We want that to be fulfilled but we don't belong to any group, and it's in the big cities and so on that the really heartless behaviour seems to take place.

A I'm sure that being in cities is part of it, and certainly in the first story that must be a major part of it, the fact that you feel that there are, the institutions are already set up whereby people are going to be protected, the police will do something.

C You had an example of that football the attack of the footballer. (Yes) And what was the reaction of the people standing round, did they just ...?

A Nobody did anything. Yes. A footballer attacked the crowd, which was a very unusual situation and nobody, nobody did anything.

- Elicit some conditional constructions and any other useful vocabulary and encourage students to use these to discuss question **3**.

Writing

- 'Charity begins at home.' Discuss.

2 Are you an altruist?

- Students do quiz individually and then predict what they think their partner would do in such situations. They then compare their predictions with their partner.

Writing

- Students write their own quiz and then ask partner their invented questions.

Kindness

1 Love thy neighbour

A young woman, called Kitty Genovese, was walking along the streets of a middle-class neighbourhood in New York at 3.00 am, when she was attacked. She screamed for help and managed to escape. A few minutes later her assailant caught her again and she continued screaming for half an hour whilst 38 neighbours watched transfixed from their windows and did nothing. They didn't even call the police. Kitty died of multiple stab wounds.

In another town in America, a man went to a garage sale and bought an old tool box for $15. At home when he opened it up, he found $5,500 hidden under some plates at the bottom of the box. He returned the money to the woman he'd bought the box from. ■

1 Which seems to be the strangest story – Kitty Genovese's or the man returning the money?

2 What do you think? True or False?

People did nothing to help Kitty because they:

(a) prefer to protect themselves rather than get involved and risk being killed.

(b) no longer have a group or tribal feeling which binds them together – we are all too individual and we always put ourselves first.

(c) convince themselves that there are already institutions in cities to deal with this kind of problem; they don't need to intervene because the police will intervene for them.

(d) basically selfish and just don't care about other people.

The man returned the box because:

(e) he was a noble altruist.

(f) he was simply afraid he might have been caught.

3 What would you do in the following situations?

(a) You see someone suspicious hanging around outside a neighbour's door.

(b) You see a teenager stealing some sweets from a shop? (And if it was a little old lady?)

(c) You see someone of a different colour skin being beaten up by four of your colour skin.

(d) You see a mother violently beating her screaming child.

(e) You see some children teasing and taunting another child.

2 Are you an altruist?

1 You see an old lady struggling to cross the street with some heavy bags.
- a You ignore her, she should get herself a shopper's trolley.
- b You help her to cross.
- c You help her to cross and then offer to carry her bags home for her, even though she lives in the opposite direction.

2 At a party there's one more chocolate left on the plate.
- a You take it and eat it when no one's looking.
- b You offer it to the others first.
- c You insist that someone else have it, though your mouth is watering.

3 You run over a cat in your car/on your bike.
- a You carry on driving.
- b You stop and knock at the presumed owner's door.
- c After calming down the owner you offer to take the cat to the vet.

4 A neighbour's car alarm goes off in the middle of the night.
- a You close the window and put your ear plugs in.
- b You ring the neighbour but do nothing more if there's no reply.
- c You rush round to investigate.

5 You are driving along a country road in the dead of night. A bedraggled person of unknown sex tries to flag you down.
- a It's probably some drunken maniac.
- b You drive past and feel terribly guilty that you didn't stop.
- c You stop immediately and give whatever assistance is needed.

Score: If the majority of your answers are As: You are thoroughly selfish, but definitely part of the great indifferent majority. Bs: You do your bit to help the world, though rather half-heartedly. Cs: You're on a one-way ticket to heaven.

3 Mother Teresa of Calcutta

- Elicit names of people who appear to be motivated by pure altruism. Elicit Mother Teresa. Find out how much students already know about her, encouraging them to talk about the aspects mentioned in the listening.

Listening

- Students hear a brief history of the life of Mother Teresa and answer some very simple questions.
  Questions: **1** Where and when was she born? **2** Who was her father? **3** Where was her first missionary work? **4** When did she move to Calcutta? **5** When did she win the Nobel Peace Prize? **6** How many saris does she possess?

1 *Serbia, 1910* **2** *rich merchant* **3** *Ireland* **4** *1928* **5** *1979* **6** *two*

One person who no one could really accuse of having ulterior motives for helping others is Mother Teresa of Calcutta. She was born in Serbia in 1910. Her father was a rich merchant who gave generously to the church and fed the poor at his table. She did very well at school and spurred on by her father's example, she decided to become a missionary. She joined the Order of Loreto nuns in Ireland and then moved to Calcutta in 1928. She opened a house for the dying, another one for abandoned babies and established medical services for lepers. Later she opened centres around the world and as a result of this work won the Nobel Peace Prize in 1979. Since then her work in Calcutta has been interspersed with visits to various disaster victims around the world – from the Bhopal pollution victims to those of the Armenian earthquake. Her only possessions are two white saris, a bucket in which to wash and her devotional books.

- Students now look at the statements on their page and discuss whether the first statement is true of Mother Teresa. They then discuss the other statements. For statements **1** and **4** you could ask students to think of other well-known people who do charitable work, then lead the discussion on to how the media presents such people to us.

Not everyone sees Mother Teresa as a saintly figure. In 1995 a TV documentary suggested she had been receiving money from dubious sources.

Writing

- Students choose one of these titles: (a) If everyone spent one hour a day helping someone worse off than themselves, the world would be a better place. Discuss. (b) Every human being deserves a share of the world's resources. Discuss.

4 The Red Cross

- Before beginning exercise, brainstorm students on what the Red Cross is, and how and when it was founded. With a membership of 250,000,000 people, you might even have a member in your class.
- Students then read text. Brainstorm question **1** as a whole class activity. Then in groups they discuss question **2**.

2 a *Apart from wartime activities this is probably the most well-known form of aid that the Red Cross offers.*
b *These are money raising activities as the Red Cross is a self-financed charity.*
c *One of the tragedies of war and natural disasters is the separation of families. Using its worldwide network centred in Geneva the Red Cross is constantly striving to reunite families, no matter how long the separation. The British Red Cross, for example, manages to trace, on average, one person every day of the year.*
d *Again in war or natural disasters, many people are cut off from the families because normal communications have broken down. Relatives may be taken prisoner-of-war or moved to refugee camps or shelters. In these circumstances the Red Cross Message Service is often the only means for families to keep in touch.*
e *The Cosmetic Camouflage service aims to help people cope with disfigurement and blemishes, including scars, birthmarks and conditions such as vitiligo. The Red Cross also offers beauty care techniques for the blind. Volunteers demonstrate to women with impaired vision how to apply their make-up. The service is intended to give confidence to visually handicapped people, offer independence and provide an interest which can be shared with other women.*

3 Mother Teresa of Calcutta

1 Nobody does something for nothing.

2 I would never give money to charity.

3 There's no point in giving money to beggars, they only spend it on alcohol.

4 Events like Band Aid are motivated by publicity rather than humanity.

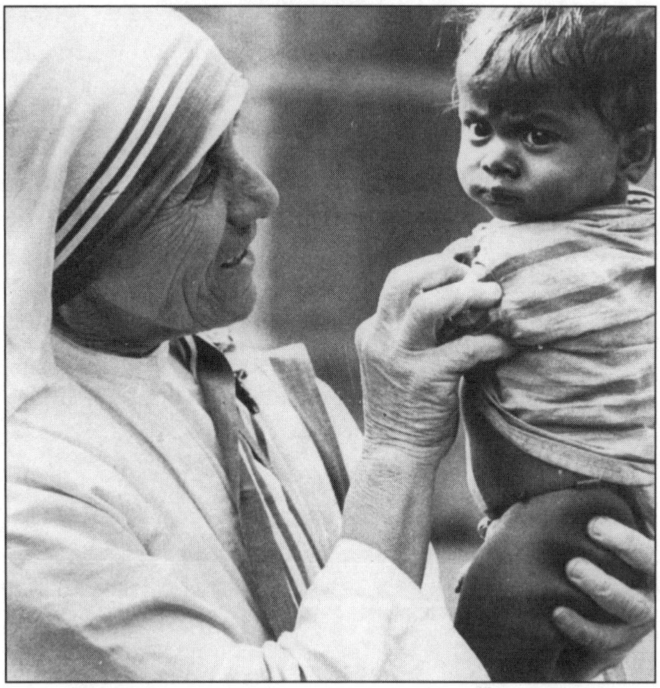

4 The Red Cross

1 Why is it important that the Red Cross is a totally independent non-political organisation?

2 Which of the following services do you think the Red Cross offers and why does it offer them?
(a) First aid at sporting and public events.
(b) Working in shops, organising bazaars and car-boot sales.
(c) Tracing separated families.
(d) Message sending.
(e) Beauty care.

***In 1859** a young Swiss businessman saw something which was to change his life and influence the course of history. The young man was Henry Dunant who witnesses the carnage following the Battle of Solferino, in Italy. He was deeply moved by the dreadful suffering of the wounded from both sides who were left largely uncared for.*

This appalling scene was the birthplace of a magnificent human idea. Henry saw every country creating a body of trained volunteers who would care impartially for the wounded of all sides, protected by international agreement. His vision led directly to the founding of the Red Cross, the signing of the First Geneva Convention, and the adoption of the Red Cross, and later the Red Crescent, as an international symbol of protection.

Today the International Red Cross and Red Crescent Movement is the world's largest voluntary organisation, with a global membership close to 250,000,000, and a National Society in almost every country of the world.

Love

Warm-ups

- Brainstorm students on different types of love (not just for people, but for nations, places, things, activities) and different ways of showing love.
- Students write a list of three things they love and hate doing. They then read their list to their partner who has to guess if it's love or hate.

1 The things we do for love

- Students read the text (fictional). Then ask them to read and tick the items **1–7** that they themselves would do for love. Then proceed to the listening.

Listening

- Students hear two friends talking about what they would do for love in relation to the questions that students have just answered. Their task is to understand which of questions **1–7** are asked and whether the answer is yes or no.

4 *yes* **2** *no* **1** *no*

- Get class feedback to find out if any students were prepared to do all the things for love.

A Laurelie. It seems incredible that you've been with Pete for five years.

B Can you believe it?

A Yes, I know. Well, I remember you always used to say that you would do anything for him, absolutely anything, now do you still think so?

B Those were the early days, you always say things like that.

A Exactly, but I'm asking you now, five years on, would you do anything for him?

B No, not anything obviously, there are things I wouldn't do, one just the other night, I said 'forget it'. Like what? Like what? Give me an example.

A OK right, now let's think. Now, if um, OK, say he was wanted by the police, would you lie to protect him?

B Ooh, it'd depend on the crime I think. If it was a traffic ticket, probably. But no, ooh. Yes, I probably would actually even if it was a serious one – isn't that terrible? I just realised that about myself. Yes, I probably would, unless, of course, he did something to me.

A Right. OK, well we'll leave that one. What about career, would you give up your career, if he wanted you to give up your job would you do that?

B No, why could he possibly want me to give it up?

A Well, I don't know, say if he was feeling threatened by your success or something like that.

B No, absolutely not.

A But he might be (yes he might be), what if he really wanted you to give up your career would you?

B Of course not. Not for that reason no, because that would break us up eventually because of the resentment, I wouldn't ask him to give up his career, unless he changed careers and I don't know, (OK OK) became a hit man or something.

A What about if he, say if he found a new religion or something, that he was completely obsessed with and he wanted you to convert to that religion, would you do that for him?

B He's a good Catholic boy I somehow can't see that happening. You mean like some cult or something? That I think would be the beginning of the end. If someone's obsessive about religion I think that there's only room for that.

A But if you loved him? And that was part of him.

B I'd let him go to his god.

2 Marriage contracts

- Do the **The things we do for love** section first.
- Listen to the extract and brainstorm students on what a marriage contract might be and what clauses might be in it. Finally, students read the passage for confirmation of what came up during the class discussion.

B If I ever got married I think I'd have to have some kind of a pre-nuptial agreement written up.

A What do you mean?

B You know, a pre-nuptial agreement, well, a kind of a marriage contract where both partners would have to stipulate exactly what they were prepared to give up for the other one and how far they were prepared to go…

ⓘ A number of famous people have or have had marriage contracts – Henry VIII, Mick Jagger (with Bianca), Aristotle Onassis with Jackie Kennedy. This practice is also quite common with modern French couples.

1 The things we do for love

Some people, it seems, would do just

anything for their loved one...

Roberto Filippi, a 27-year-old Italian man, became obsessed by a girl he saw on the Milan metro. Everyday as he took the 8.23 train to the Duomo, Roberto watched his loved one from a distance, until one day he found the courage to present her with some flowers on the return train back to the suburbs.

She appreciated the gesture and they were soon going out together. It wasn't long before she, Lorella, moved town, and of course Roberto had to give up his job to follow her. Then it was election time, and Lorella managed to persuade Roberto, a lifelong communist, to vote against his instincts, for a neo-Fascist party. Soon after that, Lorella was arrested for a suspected racial attack, but she got Roberto to swear in court that she had in fact been with him on the night in question. A few months later, to escape another prosecution, Lorella left for the United States, and naturally, like a faithful dog, Roberto followed her. In America, Lorella quickly became involved in a satanic cult. When Lorella asked Roberto if he'd be prepared to act as a human sacrifice, for the first time in their relationship he managed to say 'no'.

So, what would you do for your loved one? Would you

1 change your religion?

2 give up your career?

3 emigrate?

4 tell a lie to the police to protect him/her?

5 give up your friends?

6 break all ties with your family?

7 vote against your conscience in a political election?

2 Marriage contracts

It is becoming increasingly common for couples about to be married to sign a pre-nuptial agreement. This agreement is drawn up by lawyers and is aimed at avoiding possible disagreements during the marriage and to avoid contention during a possible divorce. The couples individually stipulate what they feel is important in terms of day-to-day living, such as how much money should be spent on food, going out, hobbies etc.; how domestic responsibilities should be divided up e.g. who does the cooking, who cleans the bathroom; who looks after the children; and whether it is possible for partners to take separate holidays. Having such a contract means that if such an issue should arise then at least there's a good basis for a reasonable discussion. The divorce clauses basically deal with who gets what should the marriage not work out.

3 Are you a good lover?

- Students answer true or false to the questions and discuss them in groups.
- They then discuss different attitudes to love deciding which questions indicate (a) a romantic approach to love (b) a realistic approach and (c) a cynical approach. This should enable them to write a score/analysis for the test. Finally, they can compare their analyses with those of other groups.

Writing

- Students choose one of these titles: (a) It is better to have loved and lost than never to have loved at all. Discuss. (b) All is fair in love and war. Discuss.

4 A kiss is just a kiss?

- Brainstorm students on how they give formal kisses in their country, i.e. where on the face, how many times, and what it means. Students then read the text and discuss statements.

ⓘ The article says people kiss twice in France, but a lot of French actually kiss three times.

Love

3 Are you a good lover?

1 *Love* is an art which needs to be learned if it is to be practised well.

2 You can *love* someone too much.

3 A man and woman can be really good friends without being in *love*.

4 Women have deeper relationships with same-sex friends than men.

5 Men are more attracted to women who are hard to get.

6 Women should never make the first move.

7 You cannot be truly in *love* with two people at the same time.

8 You should only have eyes for your *lover*.

9 It is impossible to *love* and be wise.

10 *Love* can never be forever.

4 A kiss is just a kiss?

While the language of love-making may be universal when two people are from the same culture, the act of kissing can mean very different things in different parts of the world.

In China for example, kissing someone in public is seen as unhygienic and repulsive. In Japan, it may be tolerated, but only if the couple stand with bodies well apart and lips shut tight. And the Inuits of Alaska wouldn't dream of doing anything more oral than rubbing noses – not out of any moral scruples but because Inuit women tend to use their mouths for more everyday tasks such as cleaning oil lamps and chewing animal hides to soften them up.

Even if your intentions aren't amorous, you can still run into trouble. Many a foreigner has come unstuck when greeting a friend who is Dutch (mandatory three cheek-pecks) or French (two only).

1 Men kissing each other is disgusting.

2 Shaking hands is the best way to greet someone.

3 Kissing relatives is always embarrassing.

4 Scenes from films which show lovers kissing should be cut.

5 Couples should not be allowed to kiss in the street, on the bus, at the cinema, at school, at work.

Money

Warm-ups

- In a mixed nationality class, ask students to bring in coins and notes from their countries. Students then compare their currencies and try to set the parameters for ideal coins and notes. Factors involved: **1** notes: number of denominations + related colour and differences; aesthetics, size **2** coins: shape, weight, size, aesthetics, help for the blind

- Students imagine they have been given £1m to be spent in a specific way. In groups they prepare a project. Possible tasks: to improve their town (in monolingual classes); to design and build a dream house; to start their own business; to invent a new machine; to spend it all in a week without buying anything. If each group is given the same task they can then compare their solutions.

1 Money makes the world go around

Listening

- Students listen to a short history of the uses of, and alternatives to, money. Their task is to decide which of the pictures of alternatives to money on their page are mentioned. They should also understand how money has been used not only as a method of payment.

Really, anything which is accepted can be used as money, and many items over the centuries have served this purpose. American Indians have used beads made from shells; in India, cowrie shells, and in the Fiji islands, whale teeth; the early colonists of North America utilised tobacco; cigarettes and liquor were used after the Second World War in Germany, and some southern Europeans used sweets as small change. Today, in some holiday camps plastic beads made into bracelets and necklaces are used instead of money; and tokens are of course a common substitute in slot machines.

The wide use of cattle in primitive times survives in the word 'pecuniary' from the Latin 'pecus' meaning cattle; and the word 'salary' reminds us of how the Roman soldiers used to be paid in salt. Coins began to be employed on a regular basis in the seventh century in a Greek state in Asia Minor. Originally they were very heavy and were made of a mixture of silver and gold. In this period coins were also used to spread propaganda about the power of the ruler whose head was shown on the face of the coin. Coins were also used as amulets and for decorative purposes. The use of paper money only began about 200 years ago.

- On the basis of the information in the listening, in small groups, students then answer question **1**.

Possible disadvantages of some of the alternatives: deterioration, transportation difficulties, difficult to split up, impossible to accumulate (i.e. no savings), not scarce enough

- Then brainstorm the whole class on questions **2** and **3**. Alternatively, in groups, students think of as many consequences as possible in five minutes. See which group can provide the longest list. Ask students how they would pay for their English lessons, i.e. what they could offer in exchange. One advantage of bartering is that it avoids inflation, and it might be a little more difficult to amass great wealth.

2 Will you ever be rich?

- Before doing the quiz, brainstorm students on the following questions: How do people get rich? Who deserves to be rich? What do the rich do? How does money affect and change people?
- Students now do the quiz and discuss their answers, inventing (if they wish) their own scoring system. Then get them to write three more questions to ask other members of the class (either in their group or by walking round the classroom). In a whole class activity students vote on the best questions.

Writing

- Students discuss one of the following titles: (a) 'Money is the root of all evil.' (b) Would you rather be rich and stupid, or poor and intelligent?

Listening

- Students listen to a totally over-the-top woman being interviewed on how she became so fantastically rich and answer these questions.
(The tapescript is on page 58.)
Questions: **1** True or false? Dolores was born in the USA **2** T or F? D enjoys swimming in champagne. **3** How many times has she been married? Is she married now? **4** T or F? Dolores' first husband was 60 years older than her. **5** T or F? Many newspapers have had to give Dolores a lot of money for printing supposedly libellous stories about her. **6** What other methods has Dolores used to get money? **7** What is her dream?

1 *F* **2** *T* **3** *eight times, not currently married* **4** *F* **5** *T* **6** *fires, husbands' life insurances, insurance on jewellery* **7** *to rob a bank*

Money

1 Money makes the world go around

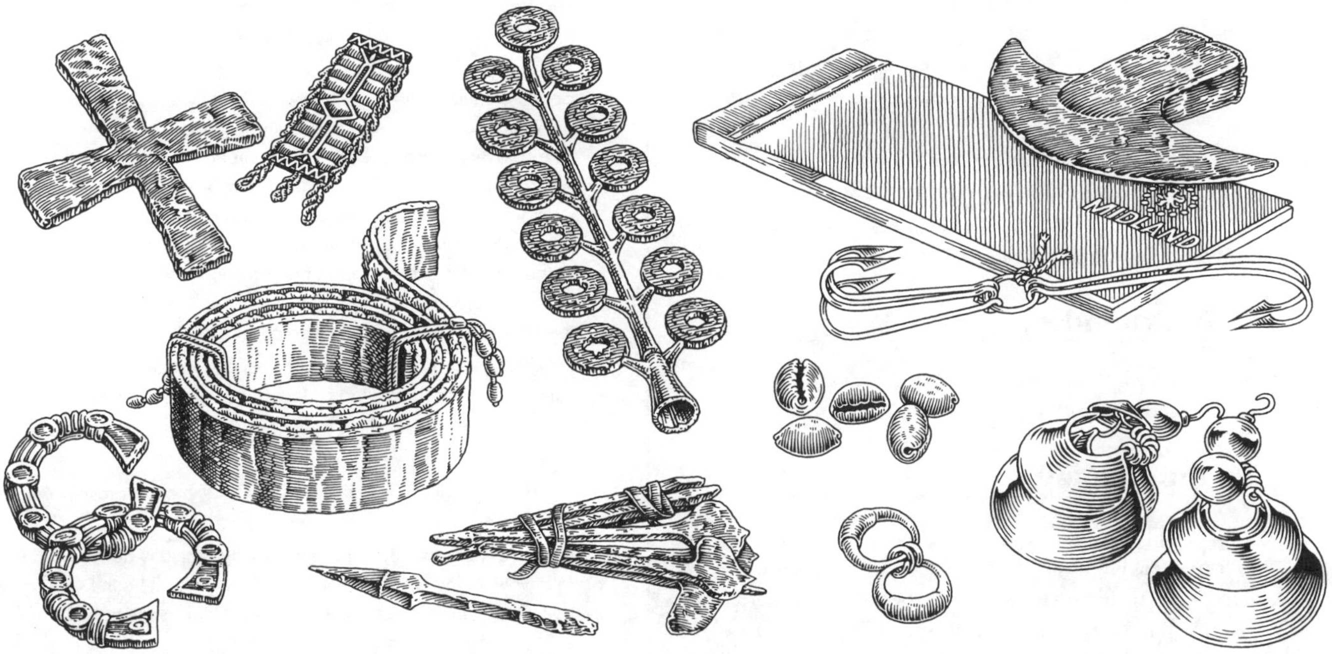

1 What are the advantages and disadvantages of some of the alternatives to our idea of money mentioned in the listening exercise and of those shown in the pictures above?

2 What would be the consequence of a world without money? Would there be no poverty?

3 What are the advantages of using a bartering system?

2 Will you ever be rich?

THE 'Will you ever be rich?' test

BY IVOR FORTUNE

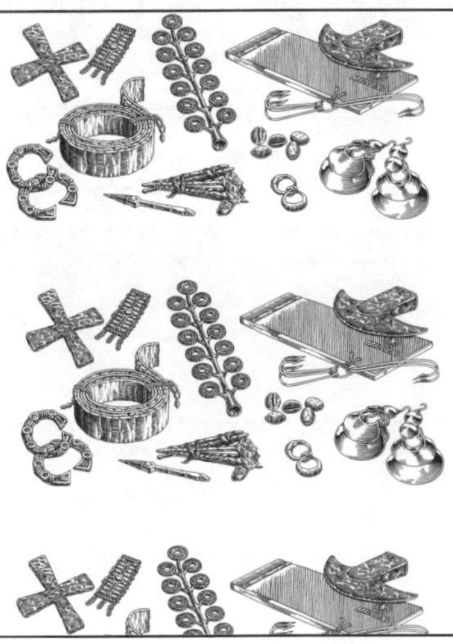

1 Someone asks you to lend them $5. Do you ...
- (a) refuse?
- (b) lend them the $5?
- (c) lend them $50, as they are more likely to remember to pay you back?

2 After one week, they haven't returned your $5. Do you ...
- (a) bring the matter up casually in conversation?
- (b) demand your money back?
- (c) forget it?

... And what would you do if it was a book instead of money?

3 You win $1m in a lottery. Do you ...
- (a) invest it?
- (b) give most of it to charity?
- (c) go on a spending spree?

4 You find a wallet full of dollars. Do you ...
- (a) hand it in to the police?
- (b) if possible, contact the owner?
- (c) pocket the money?

5 You haven't had a raise in salary/pocket money etc. for a long time. Do you ...
- (a) confront your boss/parents?
- (b) make gentle hints?
- (c) wait for them to bring the subject up?

Money

3 Everyone has their price

- Students discuss what money can't buy. Possible contenders (some of which obviously can be bought): health, children, happiness, youth, a clear conscience, other people's love and feelings, freedom. Students now discuss the questions.

Alternatively, show Robert Redford's $1m question in the film *Indecent Proposal*. You may like to invent a whole range of related questions with the right kind of group, but be careful not to offend anyone.

4 Backhanders

- Do this as a whole class exercise. It could lead to a discussion on political corruption.

5 Your money

- Students fill in the grid and discuss their percentages with their partner. Tell students that there is no need for the percentages to add up to exactly 100 per cent, but merely to be a rough indication of how they spend their money.
- In multilingual classes this might lead to a discussion on spending and saving habits around the world.

Tapescript for **2 Will you ever be rich?**

P = presenter I = interviewer D = Dolores

P Good evening and welcome to 'Mind Your Pennies'. In tonight's edition we'll be talking to a farmer whose hens lay golden eggs, and to a child whose tooth fairy apparently left him 10 million dollars under his pillow. But first, the woman women love to hate, Dolores Mint, is going to give us some hints on how to become rich without working. For the few who don't know, Dolores 'Dollar' Mint was born in poverty in a small town on the Mexican border. Her determination to survive led her to cross the border at the age of 13 and to work her way up to Hollywood. Now, recently widowed for the eighth time, we went to visit Dolores by the side of her champagne-filled swimming pool.

I Dolores you are now quoted in Fortune magazine as being America's tenth richest lady. How did you achieve this?

D Well of course I picked my men right. They were all very wealthy and, well, extremely old.

I If I remember right, your first husband was more than sixty years older than you.

D I was 16, he was 60, so no, not exactly. Actually he was relatively young. But the others, well, they've all been like what you'd call senior citizens, who have had this nasty habit of dying or divorcing me soon after I married them.

I But marrying the right men hasn't been your only source of income has it?

D Many of my marriages, or more my divorces I should say, and of course the sudden deaths, have attracted a lot of publicity, and newspapers have said the most libellous things, suggesting that I only married them for their money, and that I even murdered some of them.

I Whatever could possibly have made them think that?

D I just don't know. But the fact is I've made a fortune in suing people and in various libel suits. I've also had some fun with insurance companies.

I In what sense?

D Well my husbands have always given me very expensive jewels, which I just have this terrible habit of losing, and then when the insurance money comes, they just miraculously reappear.

I And then of course there's the fires.

D Yes, well let's not go into that. There have only been three and to be honest the compensation was minimal, but my husbands' life insurances have come in handy.

I I'm sure. Well thank you very much Dolores – it's all been most enlightening and I'm sure you've given our listeners some food for thought. But before you go there's just one question I'd like to ask – with the fantastic life you've led, with all the famous people you've met, is there anything you haven't done that you'd just love to do?

D Yes, rob a bank.

3 Everyone has their price

What would you do for the right price and assuming that you really needed the money?

1 Disclose confidential company secrets.

2 Testify falsely in court while under oath.

3 Try out a drug being experimented by a pharmaceutical company.

4 Donate unnecessary parts of your body to an unknown patient.

5 Kill someone you'd never met and who you were convinced was dangerous.

4 Backhanders

Would you try and bribe someone for money in any of the following circumstances?

1 The waiter to get you and your wonderful new partner the best table in the restaurant.

2 Your teacher to let you see an examination paper in advance.

3 The tax inspector so that you don't have to pay huge amounts of taxes.

4 A personnel manager to give you a job.

5 The police to avoid a speeding fine.

5 Your money

What proportion of your income do you allocate to the following? Try and give a rough percentage, e.g. 0%, 5%, 15%, 25+%.

	%		%		%
books		gambling		music + videos	
car/travel expenses		hairdressers, beautician, etc.		rent/mortgage	
care/support for family members		holidays		savings	
cinema and concerts		household bills		services of other people (cleaners, gardeners, etc.)	
clothes		insurance		sport + fitness	
food		medical			

1 What things would you like to spend more/less on?

2 What's the most expensive thing you've bought recently?

3 What thing do you most regret having bought?

4 Are you saving up to buy anything in particular?

5 How have your spending habits changed over the last ten years?

6 Is talking about money a taboo subject in your country?

Numbers

Warm-up

- Introduce the expression 'Two's company, three's a crowd', using this joke: 'If two is company and three is a crowd, what are four and five?' (Answer: nine!) Then ask students to discuss the ideal number of: **(a)** students in a class **(b)** guests at a wedding **(c)** friends for a dinner **(d)** working days per week **(e)** weeks of holiday **(f)** hours of homework per day **(g)** friends to go with to the cinema. For the listening exercise (see below) to be successful, students must discuss at least **c**, **d** and **g**. This exercise could be done as a walk-around activity, with each student being given a particular question to ask fellow students. The results could be written down in the form of a statistical analysis.

Listening

- Students listen to three people answering some of the questions **(a)–(g)**. Students have to identify which subject is being talked about, and what the ideal number is.

1 (c) *dinner party, eight* **2 (c)** *dinner party (probably) – three or four* **3 (g)** *cinema – alone* **4 (d)** *every day for a good job, none for a bad job*

1 I love to entertain and when I was a child I read a novel, might have been by Somerset Maugham, in which a character said that eight was the perfect number for a dinner party, because it was intimate enough to allow general conversation, but large enough to have a feeling of a party.

2 If they're very close friends that's very nice if there are just three or four of you. (Yeah)

3 I know my ideal number for going to the cinema though, any cinema audience the ideal number is me (yes I agree with you) and nobody else.

4 My uncle always used to say, and I'm sure he was quoting someone else, that if you find a job you love you'll never work another day in your life and I kind of feel like that, cos as long as there's variety I'm quite happy to work every day. (In any horrible job, the ideal number of working days would be none.)

1 The origin of counting

- Students read text and discuss questions in groups.

(2) The most obvious advantages of 12 over 10, is that 12 can be more easily divided (12: 2, 3, 4 and 6; 10: 2, 5). 12 is also related to the way we calculate time. **(3)** Calculations must have been difficult. **(4)** They are used to subdivide documents; they are often found at the end of TV programmes to indicate the year of production. **(5)** cardinal = one, two; ordinal = first, second.

2 How many?

Listening

- In this exercise students hear some statistics about languages. You can approach this in two ways depending on the level. With lower levels, students guess the answers to the questions, individually and then in groups – obviously they can only be guesses. Then tell them to listen for the answers on the tape. With higher levels, before you make the photocopies, blank out the numbers on the student's page. In groups first ask students to guess the answers, then to write down the numbers as they hear them on the cassette. Obviously you will need to play the tape several times. Very good listeners might like to write down some of the other statistics.

1 *5000* **2** *350m* **3** *350m; 2,382,509* **4** *194–214* **5** *615,000* **6** *1,913*

There are about five thousand languages in the world, and the one with the most speakers is Mandarin, with about six hundred and fifty million speakers. English has around three hundred and fifty million speakers.

The most common surname in the world is Chang of whom there are about three hundred and fifty million. Smith is the most common English surname: there are around eighty thousand in England and Wales, and an estimated two million, three hundred and eighty two thousand five hundred and nine in the United States.

Some languages are more complex than others. Tillamook, the North American Indian language has the most prefixes with thirty. Eskimo uses sixty three forms of the present tense and simple nouns have as many as two hundred and fifty inflections. English has between one hundred and ninety four and two hundred and fourteen irregular verbs depending on what you define as an irregular verb.

The largest dictionary in the world is the *Oxford English Dictionary*, which has twenty volumes, twenty one thousand seven hundred and twenty eight pages, two hundred and ninety thousand five hundred main entries, and around fifty nine million words. It lists the definitions of around six hundred and fifteen thousand words. The *Webster's International Dictionary*, the American equivalent of the *Oxford English Dictionary*, lists four hundred and fifty thousand words. Though in both cases technical and scientific terms would add millions more. Altogether about two hundred thousand English words are in common use.

The longest word in English has one thousand nine hundred and thirteen letters, and is the chemical name for a protein.

Numbers

1 The origin of counting

Although primitive men had little difficulty in judging quantities by naming individual members or items of a group, they weren't, as such, able to count them and would be unable to make the connection between say three leaves and three apples.

Anthropologists assert that counting methods were extremely basic, with words for 'one' and 'two' and then a word which just meant 'many' (much the same as today we talk about 'crowds' of people, 'herds' of animals, and 'handfuls' of sweets). As recently as 1972, a tribe of cave-dwellers in the Philippines couldn't answer the question 'How many people are there in your tribe?', although they could individually list all 24 members of their group. And one tribe who lives on the fringes of the Amazon jungle, even today, has no system of numbers, merely a verb meaning 'to be two alike'.

Some languages still preserve a distinction between one, two and many, in what is grammatically known as the 'dual form'. In Arabic for example 'bait' means 'house' and 'baiten' means 'two houses'. Similar forms exist in the pronoun 'you', where there is a distinction between you singular, you two and you many.

The earliest counting system, binary, was also based on this one two system. Hands and fingers were used to express both numbers and measurements, and the fact that we have ten fingers probably accounts for the development of the decimal system, though this doesn't explain the English and American aversion to such a system (one theory is that they originally had 12 fingers!)

The actual writing of numbers progressed from using notches through to symbols. The Arabic system of numbers is now the most widely used, with Roman numerals being for more specialized use.

1. In your language do you have any equivalents of the 'dual form'?
2. Analyse the advantages of the 12 system over the decimal system and vice versa.
3. What problems must the Romans have had with their system?
4. What are the specialised uses of Roman numerals today?
5. Could we manage with just cardinal numbers, rather than having both cardinal and ordinal?

2 How many?

1. How many languages do you think there are in the world?
   50; 500; 5,000; 50,000
2. How many native English speakers are there?
   (in millions) 315; 350; 415; 450
3. Smith and Chang are two very common surnames.
   How many Changs are there in the world?
   (in millions) 30; 35; 315; 350
   How many Smiths are in the USA?
   18,000; 80,000; 2,302,509; 2,382,509
4. How many irregular verbs are there in English?
   94; 194; 214; 240
5. How many words are defined in the Oxford English Dictionary?
   415,000; 450,000; 615,000; 650,000
6. How many letters does the longest English word have?
   13; 30; 1,913; 1,930

3 Numerology

- Students first read the text, then before calculating their number they should read the analysis and decide which description best describes them. They should then calculate their number and see if the real description coincides with the one they'd previously chosen.

ⓘ People actually believe in this, and even calculate the effects that a name change (e.g. Reg Dwight to Elton John) can have on the personality of that person.

4 Is there any logic in it?

- In groups of four, give students ten minutes to answer as many questions as possible. The group which answers the most questions is the winner.

1 *one* **2** *one* **3** *three* **4** *eight – He makes seven to start with, smokes them and then he makes the eighth from their ends.* **5** *four hours – You take the first pill straight away, not after half an hour.* **6** *None. The ladder of course rises as the tide rises.* **7** *left 7, right 5*

- Write the number 7 and the word 'red' on a piece of paper and tell students you are going to predict their answers in a psychological test. Ask students rapidly and repeatedly the following questions: 'Five times five', 5x6, 6x6 etc.' and then say: write down a colour and a number between 5 and 10. Most students will write 7 and 'red' at which point you reveal your prediction, although there seems to be no rational explanation for this.

Numbers

3 Numerology

Had enough of astrology? Another way to delve into the depths of your personality is through *numerology*, a very pseudo-science which has formulated simple rules for calculating your 'lucky' number, This number will then tell you all about *your character*. In one system, the number is calculated from the letters of your first name, with each letter corresponding to a number. These numbers are then summed to produce your lucky number. Use the system below and then see what your lucky number means. If your number exceeds nine, e.g. 10 or 18, simply add these digits together (10 = 1+0 =1, 18 =1+8=9)

1	2	3	4	5	6	7	8	9
A	B	C	D	E	F	G	H	I
J	K	L	M	N	O	P	Q	R
S	T	U	V	W	X	Y	Z	

EXAMPLE: A D R I A N = 1+4+9+9+1+5 = 29 (2+9) = 11 (1+1) = **2**

ANALYSIS

1 Creative, inventive, positive, ambitious. **Lucky day**: Sunday. **Favourite colour**: gold, yellow.
2 Gentle, imaginative, romantic, more mental than physical. **Lucky day**: Monday, Friday. **Favourite colour**: green, white.
3 Ambitious, proud, a little dictatorial. **Lucky day**: Thursday. **Favourite colour**: mauve, purple.
4 Rebellious, antisocial, not very successful in life. **Lucky day**: Saturday. **Favourite colour**: half shades/tones e.g. grey, beige.
5 Highly strung, impulsive, resilient, sociable, risk-taking. **Lucky day**: Wednesday, Friday. **Favourite colour**: grey, white.
6 Romantic, popular, loyal, try to promote happiness. **Lucky day**: Tuesday. **Favourite colour**: blue.
7 Independent, individualistic, love travel and learning. **Lucky day**: Monday. **Favourite colour**: green, white.
8 Lonely, misunderstood, this is an unlucky number. **Lucky day**: Saturday. **Favourite colour**: black.
9 Determined, resent criticism, exaggerated self-esteem. **Lucky day**: Tuesday. **Favourite colour**: red.

4 Is there any logic in it?

1 There is a small oil slick in the middle of a lake. Every day it doubles in size. After 64 days it covers half the lake. How many more days will it take before it covers the whole lake?

2 A farmer had two and a half haystacks in one corner of a field, and three and a half haystacks in another corner of the same field. If he put them all together how many haystacks would he have?

3 A little girl is getting dressed to go to a birthday party. Her mother has bought her a new dress and she looks very pretty indeed. She is just about to take her socks out of the drawer when there's a blackout and she's left in the dark. In the drawer there are only white and black socks. How many socks will she have to pull out before getting a pair of the same colour?

4 A tramp makes his own cigarettes by collecting cigarette ends. He needs seven ends to make one cigarette. How many cigarettes can he make from 49 ends?

5 A doctor gives you nine pills and tells you to take one every half hour. How long will the pills last?

6 A rope ladder hangs over the side of a ship so that it just touches the water. Each rung is 5cm thick and there are 20cm between each rung. How many rungs will be under water by the time the tide has risen 1m?

7 Superman always goes around with a load of chewing gum in his pockets. One day he said to Superwoman: 'If I take a piece of gum from my left trouser pocket and put it in the right one, I'll have the same number of pieces in each. But if I take a piece from the right pocket and put it in the left, I'll have twice as many pieces in the left pocket as in the right'. How many pieces of gum must he have had in each pocket?

Origins

Warm-up

- In pairs students discuss their own origins, where they were born, what they know about their ancestors, if they like their birthplace, etc.

1 Origin of the universe

- The four sentences (**1–4**) on the student's page are the beginnings and endings of the two paragraphs, **A** and **B**. Students' task is to match the beginnings and endings to the correct text.

A *4 (beginning), 2 (ending),* **B** *1, 3*

Follow-up

- Students discuss their own ideas of the origin and history of life on this planet.

2 Language

- Brainstorm students on how they think language may have begun. Students read passage then correct the animal noises in the illustrations.

baa/sheep, cock-a-doodle/cock, coo/pigeon, ee-aw/donkey, miaow/cat, moo/cow, neigh/horse, oink/pig, quack/duck, too-wit/owl.

Follow-up

- Dictate these words: creek, crunch, hum, mumble, pop, sizzle, splash, tick tock, whine, buzz. Ask students to say the words out aloud (repeating after you if necessary) and to decide what sounds these words imitate. Then do the listening.

Listening

- Students hear some of the sounds above. Their task is to match the sound to the word.

1 *creek*	**2** *mumble*	**3** *splash*	**4** *whine*	**5** *buzz*
6 *tick*	**7** *crunch*	**8** *hum*	**9** *pop*	**10** *sizzle*

Origins

1 Origin of the universe

A

A couple of hundred years ago men possessed the history of little more than the last 3,000 years. What had happened before that time was a matter of legend and speculation. Over a large part of the civilized world it was believed and taught that the world had been created suddenly in 4004 B.C., though the authorities differed as to whether this had occurred in the spring or autumn of that year.

H. G. Wells: *A Short History of the World.*

B

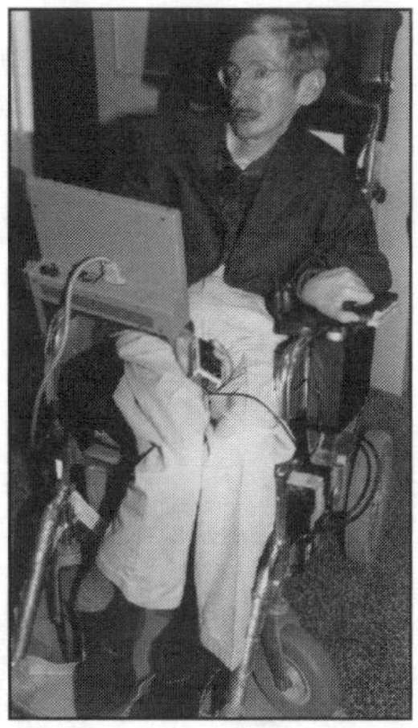

One argument for such a beginning was the feeling that it was necessary to have 'First Cause' to explain the existence of the universe. (Within the universe, you always explained one event as being caused by some earlier event, but the existence of the universe itself could be explained in this way only if it had some beginning.) Another argument was put forward by St. Augustine in his book The City of God. He pointed out that civilization is progressing and we remember who performed this deed or developed that technique.

S. HAWKING: *A BRIEF HISTORY OF TIME.*

1 According to a number of early cosmologies and the Jewish/Christian/Muslim tradition, the universe started at a finite and not very distant, time in the past.

2 This fantastically precise misconception was based upon a too literal interpretation of the Hebrew bible.

3 Thus man, and also perhaps the universe, could not have been around for that long. St. Augustine accepted a date of about 5000 B.C. for the Creation of the universe according to the book of Genesis.

4 The story of our world is a story that is still very imperfectly known.

2 Language

We will probably never know how language began, but that hasn't stopped people coming up with some weird and wonderful theories. Language began with the grunts of physical exertion claims *yo-he-ho* theory, whilst *pooh pooh* followers say it had its origins in noises associated with surprise, fear, pain and other feelings. Rhythmic primitive chanting gave rise to language according to the proponents of the *sing song* theory.

One of the most interesting theories claims that language imitates sounds (onomatopoeia). Dogs in Britain go 'bow wow', so 'bow wow' comes to mean dog. But do dogs go 'bow wow' in your country?

Origins

3 Goin' back to my roots

- Before students read the passage, in groups get them to think why people emigrate. Some possible reasons: to find work, enhance lifestyles and opportunities, improve prospects for their children (e.g. fewer class barriers), join relatives, escape persecution.
- Now use question **1** as an introduction to the reading passage. After students have read the text they then discuss the other questions.

Writing

- Students write how they imagine the story might have ended, i.e. what happened to the man when he returned to the village.

4 Firsts

- In groups, students work out and underline the first time the events took place (where and when). The answers are contained in the listening exercise.

Listening

- Students hear the answers to the 'firsts' and check their answers. They also listen for any other 'firsts' mentioned.

beauty contest (Belgium 1888); coffee drinking (Arabia 1000); diagram of flying machine (Italy 1492); electric chair (USA 1890); playing cards (China 1000); printed book (Turkestan 868, movable type Korea 1409); sandwich (England – not mentioned, 1762); phone conversation (Cuba 1849); TV transmission (England 1925); traffic lights (England 1868); + and – (Holland 1514).

Also mentioned: AIDS USA 1977; = sign England 1557; air flight USA 1903.

A ... and that was in 1911. First sandwich in 1762, by our old friend the Earl of Sandwich no less, didn't have time to interrupt his card games, so he ordered his butler to make sandwiches instead.

B Is that so? Hey, look at this: first beauty contest. Belgium in 1888. Why Belgium of all places?

A Why not? Oh, here's one I bet you're proud of. Electric chair used for the first time in 1890. Where? You've guessed it. The United States, home of democracy. Yes, you're first for Aids too, first recorded case in New York 1977. Quite a country.

B Plus and minus signs used for the first time in 1514 in Holland. Yeah well there was no way we could have guessed that one. And the equals sign, you'll be pleased to hear, was first used in Oxford in 1557. You'd have thought they'd all have been invented at the same time.

A Well, we both got this one – coffee in Arabia around 1000 AD, and just before that, playing cards in China. We were way off with the phone though – Cuba 1849.

B Cuba? I don't believe that one.

A Yes, well, it says that the inventor conversed with his invalid wife on the third floor of the building he was in.

B Sounds a likely story to me. Ah this is one I wanted to know, the first printed book: 868 in Turkestan; but the first one with movable type, whatever that is, was not until 1409 in Korea.

A Well, I got this one right. First diagram of a flying machine, was Leonardo da Vinci, as I said, in 1492.

B Yeah but the first air flight wasn't until 1903, and in the United States of course.

A But that wasn't the question was it? And England was also the first to transmit television.

B Garbage, it was the Italians.

A No, it says here, first TV transmission, London 1925. And here we are again, first traffic lights, London 1868.

B But they didn't even have cars then, so why would they have needed traffic ...

Useful further reading: *Shell book of firsts; Dictionary of science and technology* (Academic Press)

3 Goin' back to my roots

Everybody thought I was crazy even to think about going back to find my roots. I had been in New York for so long now, they said, and become so thoroughly Americanised that I would have nothing in common with people from that 'backward' Mediterranean village our family had left behind more than thirty years ago.

'You are not one of them,' warned my mother, 'they will take every dollar you have.'

'The old ladies in the village will mix you some kind of magic potion to make you fall in love with one of the village girls,' protested my aunt, 'and you'll be trapped there for life.'

'You will not be free like you are here,' added my father, 'you cannot spend more than a minute alone with a girl without compromising her reputation.'

No one could understand that I needed to go to discover who I really was. I was convinced that I could not go forward in my life without finding out and accepting where I had come from. Yet if my parents had been honest with me and told me the real reason for their emigration then I ...

1 Imagine you were returning from America to your homeland for the first time in many years, how would you feel? What would be the first things you would do? What differences would you notice? Would you see things through different eyes?

2 What must it be like to be uprooted from your homeland? How would you find living in a foreign country?

3 What advice would you give to an immigrant to your country?

4 Where do you consider to be your real 'home'? Is it important to have 'roots'? How often do you visit your birth place?

5 What conditions have led to the general feeling of 'rootlessness' in many parts of the world?

4 Firsts

WHAT?	WHERE?	WHEN?
Beauty contest	Belgium, France, Spain, USA	1778, 1888, 1928, 1968
Coffee drinking	Arabia, Brazil, Ethiopia, Turkey	1000, 1200, 1400, 1600
Diagram of flying machine	Italy, Persia, Russia, USA	1492, 1592, 1703, 1903
Electric chair	China, South Africa, USA, ex USSR	1819, 1890, 1919, 1990
Playing cards	Albania, China, India, Poland	1000, 1200, 1400, 1600
Printed book	China, Egypt, Greece, Turkestan	868 BC, 968 BC, 868, 968
Sandwich	Australia, Canada, England, S. Africa	1562, 1662, 1762, 1862
Telephone conversation	Cuba, England, Italy, Sweden	1829, 1849, 1869, 1889
TV transmission	England, Italy, Japan, Taiwan	1905, 1925, 1945, 1965
Traffic lights	Denmark, England, Germany, Uganda	1868, 1878, 1898, 1908
Use of + and – signs	Egypt, Greece, Holland, Korea	714 BC, 614, 1014, 1514

Predictions

Warm-ups

- Students write down three predictions about their classmates (or themselves – though obviously not using the first person pronoun). They can either write all three about the same person, or one for three different people. They then read out their predictions and the others have to guess who the predications relate to.

Writing

- Students write in reported speech the predictions made for them by the others, along with a comment e.g. *Adriano predicted I would get married next year – I hope he's wrong!*

1 In 1,000 years ...

- Before reading the article (a satirical piece from *The Daily Telegraph*), students write down a few predictions, serious or not, for life in 1000 years. In small groups they discuss what they have written.
- Students then read the text and in groups discuss the implications. Encourage students to think about the likelihood and consequences from various points of views – practical utility, ethics, economics, etc. Groups can then compare their analyses.

Writing

- Students choose one of the following: (a) Sketch a plan of a city in the year 2050, then write an explanation of how you imagine life will be in that city. (b) Describe a day in your life five years from now. (c) Would you rather live a thousand years into the future or back into the past?

Listening

- Students listen to an altered version of the text. (The altered parts are in *italics*.) Depending on level, they can either underline the differences, or without looking at their photocopy, try to remember the differences.

In an astonishing new book, *Your Future in the Past*, Dr Marlon *Orange*, an *Australian* pioneer in the science of futurology, examines how our entire way of life will have changed in *two thousand* years' time.

A World Tooth Bank will ensure that everybody will have a perfect set of teeth; a World *Hand* Bank will provide perfect *hands* for all; an Anti-Racial Wonder Drug will turn everybody in the world a uniform *green*, thus ending racial discrimination, war, anger, rage, unhappiness etc., at a stroke! Compulsory Space Trips for all will provide experiences of weightlessness, claustrophobia and terror which will relieve the extreme boredom of life and ensure a healthy psychological balance for *nobody*: these are only a few of the amazing changes which Dr *Orange* foresees.

2 The year 3000

Listening

- Ask students to read the six situations and simply to decide if they will come true or not. Play the first three listening extracts. Students' task is to identify which prediction is being talked about, and whether the speaker believes it will come true or not.
- Then ask them to discuss in groups what the implications would be if these situations really did come true. Get class feedback.
- With more advanced students play the fourth and fifth pieces. Again get them to identify which points are mentioned, and ask what they think about what the speakers said.

1 *d (no)* **2** *b (no)* **3** *e (not a good idea)* **4** *c (yes, already exists)* **5** *a (yes) + f (yes)*

1 Well, I know some people seem to think that we'll be taking our food in some kind of pill form, or tablets. I personally don't think that will ever happen, I think people enjoy their food too much. I think that current trends are much more to do with natural food, good foods, no preservatives etc.

2 I think there might be different ways of getting pregnant perhaps by then but I don't think men will actually be having children.

3 I don't know if it's possible, I mean I think that kind of thing is always a bit dangerous because I think that icebergs are sort of where they are for a good reason, and I think to start towing them round the world might unbalance the environment, I don't know.

4 I was saying this earlier to somebody actually. I saw something on the television about how the mind can be transmitted already by little electrical impulses from the mind on to computers and em for disabled people it's been developed, and we can make things move just by thought.

5 A Yeah, I've got to say, I think, I mean if we survive to the year 3000 the idea that there would be poor people in the year 3000 is monstrous. I mean, I don't think we'll survive till then if we carry on with the idea of having poor people and super rich people, and the two are connected.

B Do you think the world will then be such a small place as it were, that really, there'll be a sort of levelling of standards and ways of life?

A Yeah, I think the population is going to drop, as we share things better, ideas and commodities.

B So er do you think movement within all those countries will be a lot easier, no passports ...

A It might be less necessary. I think we're moving so much because we're all searching for something, and maybe we'll have found a little bit of that.

Predictions

1 In 1,000 years ...

3000

In an astonishing new book, Your past in the future, Dr Marlon Grapefruit, an American pioneer in the science of futurology, examines how our entire way of life will have changed in 1,000 years' time.

A World Tooth Bank will ensure that everybody will have a perfect set of teeth; a World Foot Bank will provide perfect feet for all; an Anti-Racial Wonder Drug will turn everybody in the world a uniform purple, thus ending racial discrimination, war, anger, rage, unhappiness etc., at a stroke! Compulsory Space Trips for all will provide experiences of weightlessness, claustrophobia and terror which will relieve the extreme boredom of life and ensure a healthy psychological balance for everybody: these are only a few of the amazing changes which Dr Grapefruit foresees. ➤

2 The year 3000

a There will be no passports and people will be able to travel and work exactly where they like.

b Men will be able to have children.

c With electronic telepathy we will be able to communicate mentally with anyone we choose.

d Most food will be in pill form.

e Icebergs will be towed to those countries needing water.

f There will be fewer people and fewer differences between rich and poor.

Predictions

3 Crystal balls?

- Before giving out photocopies, brainstorm students on various methods of fortune-telling. Write their suggestions on the board, and add any that they don't mention. Now give them their page and tell them to find which methods are illustrated.

🗝 *The illustration shows examples of: tarot cards (cartomancy), crystal ball (mirrormancy), tea leaves, dice, bumps on the head (phrenology), palms.*

- Get students to discuss whether they believe in or have tested any of these methods, if they've ever had their hand read, etc. Then move on to the statements. Against each statement they should write how probable the events are likely to be. They could also predict what they think will happen to their partner and then compare results. In any case they should discuss their solutions.

4 Fortune-telling rhymes

- Students look at the fortune-telling rhymes. Traditionally, in Britain after you have eaten a fruit pie (e.g. with plums), the number of stones left on your plate corresponds to a prediction about your wedding and future married life. Students have to match the rhyme with one of these interpretations:
1 What kind of man will you marry?
2 What kind of woman will you marry?
3 What kind of profession will you have?
4 When will you get married?
5 What transport will you use to get to the wedding?
6 What type of cloth will you wear to the wedding?
7 What will you have on your feet?
8 What kind of house will you live in?

🗝 **1** *tinker ...* **2** *lady ...* **3** *army ...* **4** *this year ...* **5** *coach ...* **6** *silk ...* **7** *boots ...* **8** *big house ...*

3 Crystal balls?

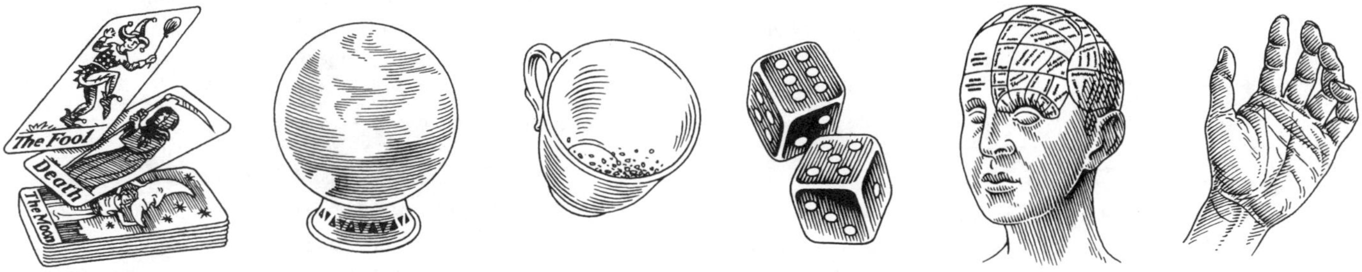

1 I will be happier in 10 years' time than I am now.

2 By the time I am middle-aged I will be much richer than my parents were at the same age.

3 In 10/20 years my best friends will still be the same as they are now.

4 My children will have a better future than me.

5 In five years I will still be doing the same job/still at the same school.

6 In 10 years I will have achieved all of my most important ambitions.

7 In 20 years my political and religious ideas will not have changed.

8 I will still be living in the same place in five years' time.

9 My love life will always be difficult.

10 In the near future I will have understood the meaning of life.

4 Fortune-telling rhymes

Lady, baby, gypsy, queen, elephant, monkey, **tangerine**

Tinker, tailor, soldier, sailor, rich man, poor man, beggarman, **thief**

Coach, carriage, wheelbarrow, **dustcart**

Silk, satin, cotton, **rags**

Army, navy, medicine, law, church, nobility, **nothing at all**

This year, next year, sometime, **never**

Boots, shoes, slippers, **clogs**

Big house, little house, pig sty, **barn**

Quizzes

1 A quiz is

- Students read the four possible origins of the word 'quiz' (question **1**). In groups they decide which is the most likely. They all refer to various uses over the last 250 years, though the *Oxford English Dictionary* claims that the word is of obscure origin and disputes the authenticity of the Dublin story.
- Students then discuss the four statements in question **2**. This could lead on to the following discussion areas: Why are women more interested in discovering their personality than men? Are men less sensitive? What are the fundamental differences between the sexes? Are TV quizzes educational or simply frivolous? Can students think of a new idea for a TV quiz game? Do students like board games like 'Trivial Pursuit'? Do they have any particularly strange quiz games in their country? What are the pros and cons of oral and written testing?

2 What would you do?

- Individually students read all the questions and think of possible answers. They then choose a few questions to ask their partner (make sure they formulate the questions correctly and don't merely say 'What do you think about question **1**?').

Listening

- Students hear several people's answers to some of the questions. Tell students that the same question may be answered by more than one person.

1 *b* **2** *c* **3** *h* **4** *i* **5** *b* **6** *e* **7** *i* **8** *a*

1 No, I wouldn't have any. I know it's easy to say so now, but I really don't think it would be fair on them.
2 This happened to me once and I was really annoyed, I mean they're obviously going to know it was you who deleted it, so you might as well tell them anyway.
3 I think I'd just forget it, but if they asked me again for some money then I'd probably remind them about the last time.
4 I'd probably swap my fork with someone else's when no one was looking, otherwise I'd deliberately drop it and ask for another one.
5 I suppose it depends on how serious the disease is, and anyway you've no way of knowing that they're going to inherit it anyway.
6 I don't think you can judge someone on one meeting only. So for the moment I wouldn't say anything and then perhaps afterwards I'd drop a few gentle hints that suggest that I wasn't too keen on this person.
7 I'd have to tell them. I can't stand eating with dirty cutlery.
8 I actually keep all my most precious things all together in case of emergencies. They're all in a little bag. So I suppose I'd just grab the bag and run.

Quizzes

1 A quiz is

1 Which of these do you think is the true origin of the word 'quiz'?

a In the eighteenth century a quiz was an odd or eccentric person, who dressed strangely and said bizarre things.

b 'Where did you get that quiz of a hat?' says a character in one of Jane Austen's novels, meaning 'where did you get that strange looking thing on your head?'

c Practical jokes in the nineteenth century were known as quizzes.

d In 1780 a Dublin theatre manager bet that within 24 hours he could introduce a new word into the English language. He went around all the walls of the town writing up his mystery word and not long after the whole town was guessing what a quiz might be. He had won his bet!

2 True or false?

a Men do more personality quizzes than women.

b Psychological tests and quizzes are meaningless.

c TV quizzes are stupid and only stupid people watch them.

d You can test someone's knowledge better by an oral test than a written test.

2 What would you do?

a Your house is on fire. You've got three minutes to save a few things.

b You have a hereditary disease and you're thinking of having children.

c You borrow someone's computer and accidentally delete something off the hard disk.

d You inherit a million pounds from an unknown relative.

e Your best friend introduces you to their new partner. The new partner is totally obnoxious.

f You are shipwrecked on a desert island. The only way to survive is by eating someone.

g Your teacher picks on you for no apparent reason.

h You lend someone $10. After two weeks they still haven't paid you back.

i At someone's house for dinner, your place has been set with a dirty fork.

j You dream that a friend of yours is going to have a terrible accident.

3 Do you agree?

- Students read all the questions individually and answer them as quickly as possible, only writing 'yes' or 'no'. Then they choose three to discuss with their group or partner. Now they can say 'it depends' providing they specify what it depends on.

Follow-up

- Students imagine that they had to answer the questions (**1–10**) as part of a job interview. In groups they discuss the following questions: **(a)** What do you think the interviewer could tell about you from the way you've answered the questions? **(b)** What do you think the 'right' answers are, or how do you think a potential employer would want the perfect employee to answer? **(c)** Do you think such tests have a valid place in interviews?
- Then students imagine that they want to join a religious group. Would they want to alter any of their answers in order to guarantee admission into the group?

4 A mix up

- Individually students first choose the most suitable answers. Then tell them that they came from three different quizzes. In groups, get them to discuss possible titles for the three quizzes.
- Now tell students that the titles are **A** 'How confident are you?', **B** 'Do you trust others?' and **C** 'How much do you think about others?' Ask them to sort out the three quizzes. Some of the questions could fit in more than one category – this is deliberate, to promote discussion. However in my own mind when I invented the quiz I did it on the basis outlined in the key.
- Finally discuss their original written answers in pairs.

🔑 **A** *3, 4, 8* **B** *1, 2, 5, 9* **C** *6, 7, 10*

3 Do you agree?

1 You learn more by reading than by taking part in a group discussion.

2 Money cannot bring happiness.

3 The best way to handle people is to tell them what they want to hear.

4 Love is more important than success.

5 Getting a good job depends mainly on being in the right place at the right time.

6 As far as world affairs are concerned, most of us are victims of forces we can neither understand nor control.

7 One should always be willing to admit mistakes.

8 The number of friends you have depends on how nice a person you are.

9 A good leader expects people to decide for themselves what they should do.

10 It is important to have traditions.

4 A mix up

1 **Which do you prefer to travel by?**
(a) train
(b) car
(c) plane

2 **You're at a restaurant where you've never been before, do you check the bill?**
(a) no
(b) of course
(c) only if it seems too high

3 **You ask someone a question and they don't answer, what do you do?**
(a) repeat the question
(b) get embarrassed and keep silent
(c) get angry

4 **Compared to other people are you ...?**
(a) better than them
(b) pretty much the same
(c) quite different

5 **A friend asks you to lend them something you really treasure, how do you feel?**
(a) rather reluctant
(b) you never lend prized possessions
(c) happy to oblige

6 **You're fifteen minutes into a long car journey towards a holiday destination with some friends. You suddenly realise you've forgotten your camera. No one else is interested in taking photos. What do you do?**
(a) ask the driver to turn round
(b) say nothing
(c) buy another camera when you arrive at your destination

7 **You're at a lecture in a foreign country which is being given by someone of your own nationality who doesn't speak the local language. The interpreter makes a crucial mistake which could lead to the audience misinterpreting your compatriot. What do you do?**
(a) say nothing
(b) intervene at the end of the lecture
(c) diplomatically interrupt the interpreter

8 **Looking six months ahead, how do you feel?**
(a) great – nothing can go wrong
(b) a bit worried
(c) indifferent

9 **You're in a train compartment with a complete stranger. You want to go to the toilet. What do you do?**
(a) take all your luggage with you
(b) just take your money
(c) leave everything there

10 **You're waiting for a bus. You overhear an ice-cream seller charging a tourist far too much for an ice-cream. What do you do?**
(a) tell the tourist
(b) smile and laugh to yourself
(c) report the ice-cream seller to the authorities

Responsibilities

Warm-ups

- Students discuss the responsibilities of the people in the relationships (**1–8**) listed below. Students should consider the responsibilities from both points of view, i.e. a company's responsibilities towards their workers and vice versa. **1** doctors and patients **2** teachers and students **3** priests and the community **4** artists and their public **5** footballers/rockstars and their fans **6** police and the community **7** politicians and the electing community **8** citizens and their nation

- Brainstorm students on jobs which demand great responsibility. Compile a list on the board, then in groups students have to rank the four most important. Possible contenders: airline pilot, army commander in chief, doctor, judge, mother, president of USA or UN, teacher. Just how responsible are such people in real life?

1 Coming of age

- Students first discuss what they think are the right ages for doing the various activities. They should then look at the ages, and try and match them with the activities. These are the ages stipulated by English law. Tell students that there are ten activities but only eight ages. This is obviously because the ages of having a child and coming home at night cannot be regulated by law – but let students themselves decide about this.

ⓘ One definition of responsibility is the ability to act or decide on one's own without supervision, which entails being able to take rational decisions and being accountable for one's own actions.

Sources seem to disagree on these ages: have a child (?), drive (17; 16 in the US), drink alcohol in a public bar (18), come home at whatever time they want (?), own a gun (15 – this should provoke some discussion), marry with parents' consent (16), buy cigarettes (16, but you can smoke at any age), vote (18), be responsible for a crime (14, no prison until 21), buy a pet (13).

Writing

- Students write about one of the following: (a) 'We are born responsible, we do not become responsible.' Discuss. (b) 'We are totally responsible for what happens in our lives – we should never blame other people or circumstances for our own mistakes and misfortunes.' Discuss.

Listening

- Students hear some people talking about what they think the right ages are. Students' task is to identify which activity is being talked about, and the age (where possible).

1 *drive, 18* **2** *drink, 18* **3** *gun* **4** *crime, 6* **5** *coming home*

1 I would, I think there's nothing wrong with em getting your licence when you're 18, which means you would learn to begin driving at about 17.

2 Oh, I think 18 is quite young enough to start drinking in a public bar.

3 I don't know that it's necessary to own a gun at all.

4 I think that anyone over the age of 6 should be responsible for a crime. Children are perfectly aware of what they are doing, if they steal something, they know they are stealing it, they know it's wrong.

5 If you want your child to be responsible I think it's a good idea to let them decide when they come home at night.

2 Criminal responsibility

- Ask students to read the two extracts, and to discuss the implications in pairs.

ⓘ **A:** This extract (based very loosely on a true story) should provoke a discussion about the expense of trials and what they actually achieve. Students should think about whether someone's circumstances and state of mind should be taken into account. For example, some legal thinkers favour trying to eliminate moral judgements about responsibility and guilt from criminal law, and concentrating on achieving its social purposes: to protect society and reform the prisoner. Students should also think about whether we should consider more the responsibility we have towards society, the victim or the criminal – do we think too much about rehabilitating the criminals rather than helping the victims?

B: This extract (from G. Gurdjieff: *Meetings with remarkable people*) should encourage a discussion about personal responsibility and at what age someone becomes responsible for their own actions. The extract implies that women become maturer earlier than men. Do students agree with this?

Writing

- 'Responsibility educates.' Discuss.

Responsibilities

1 Coming of age

be responsible for a crime

buy a pet

buy cigarettes

come home at whatever time they want

drink alcohol in a public bar

drive

have a child

marry with parents' consent

own a gun

vote

2 Criminal responsibility

A

A woman goes into a supermarket, steals a frozen chicken worth $5, puts it under her hat and is caught before she can get outside. She is taken to court. Her defence lawyer argues that she has been suffering from post-natal depression and is therefore not responsible for what she has done. The prosecution argues that no-one can put a frozen chicken under their hat without realising what they are doing. The case takes three days to resolve – the jury of twelve decide she was responsible and the judge fines her $50. Total cost of the trial? $50,000 (and that's only in terms of money, not the hours lost). It would have been much cheaper if the supermarket had just given her the chicken.

B

Until adulthood (males 20–23, females 15–19), man is not responsible for any of his acts, good or bad, voluntary or involuntary; solely responsible are the people close to him who have undertaken, consciously or owing to accidental circumstances, the obligation of preparing him for responsible life.

3 Irresponsible?

- Students read the text and read the questions without discussing them.

Listening

- Before discussing the questions, students listen to pieces **1** and **2**. Their task is to understand which questions are being talked about (the speaker is obviously being provocative).

1 *b* **2** *c*

- Students then discuss the questions in groups and then listen to pieces **3** and **4**. Their final task is to decide whether they agree with the male speaker or the female speakers.

1 I think we are responsible for our health. I'm not a smoker and I don't see why I should have to pay for smokers' illnesses. They know perfectly well that they shouldn't be smoking, I don't care how difficult it is for them to stop. My father actually stopped with three sessions of hypnotism, and he'd been smoking since the age of fourteen, so it can be done. And even if it can't be done, that's really their problem not my problem. If I decide to bash my head against the wall and then I have problems with my brain, then that's really my responsibility, I don't see it's responsibility of society.

2 I think very fat overweight people should not be given heart heart transplants. A heart transplant typically gives the patient an extra four years. The expense of the operation is phenomenally high and I think that money could be better spent, for example, on pre-natal care.

3 I think that's atrocious because a lot of smokers don't smoke because they want to any more but because they're addicted. So surely you should help them to get better anyway. Who are you to decide; you're not God.

4 I don't think withdrawing treatment should be a form of punishment. I think we should be trying to help those people who are overweight or smokers to er to get over their problem.

(**b**) Many smokers (and a few non-smokers) argue that as the government makes vast sums of money out of taxing cigarette sales then they have a moral responsibility to make amends for any negative health effects that smoking may cause. This can be countered by the fact that most governments put health warnings on cigarettes now.

4 Heaven's gates

- Tell students to rate the cases in terms of how irresponsible these people are (i.e. from least to most irresponsible). They should do this individually, and then in groups compare their answers. Students should also decide who the people are being irresponsible to.
- Alternatively, cut the sentences up into strips. Lay these face down at each group's table. Tell them that they are members of a jury at the gates of a Very Responsible Heaven. Their task is to send down the really irresponsible people to hell. One member of the group takes one of the strips of paper and says, for example, 'I am pregnant and I smoke'. This student then has to justify her/his smoking and the other members have to decide whether to send him/her down to hell. Then another student takes a strip, etc.
(I am indebted to Bob Hastings for this idea).

Extra

- Get students to look at the photos, and to discuss whether their conscience and sense of responsibility is touched by them. Get students to think about current wars, starvation crises etc. around the world. How much is their and other governments doing to help such people? And on a personal level what are they doing? Are we in any way responsible for the tragedies of other countries?

Writing

- 'Sin with the multitude, and your responsibility and guilt are as great and as truly personal as if you alone had done the wrong.' (Tyron Edwards) Discuss.

3 Irresponsible?

In a recent controversial case, a doctor refused to treat a patient whose heavy smoking had caused his health problems. The doctor felt that money was much better spent on non-smokers whose chances of long-term survival were much greater. Some doctors may have also considered refusing to treat overweight people who need heart transplants; their excess fat means that their life span may only be extended by a year or so, which, the doctors claim, hardly merits the high cost of the operation.

a How responsible are we for our health? Do we place too much reliance on government health systems and private insurance schemes?

b Should smokers be refused the same health treatment as non-smokers?

c Should overweight people be given heart transplants?

d Should fair-skinned, very frequent sunbathers (and solarium members) be refused treatment for skin cancer or at least have to pay out of their own pocket?

e Should people who participate in dangerous sports be obliged to take out health insurance rather than relying on state assistance if they have accidents?

4 Heaven's gates

1. A mother who smokes while pregnant.
2. Parents who let their children watch pornographic and violent films.
3. Someone who drives at 220 kph on the motorway.
4. People who have big dogs and live in flats.
5. A group of people climbing on a difficult mountain despite a bad weather forecast.
6. People who leave cans, plastic bottles etc. on beaches and other places of natural beauty.
7. A teacher who never prepares his/her lessons.
8. Someone who drinks a bottle of wine and then drives.
9. Producers of arms/weapons.
10. A couple of Jehovah's witnesses who refuse to let their child have a blood transfusion.

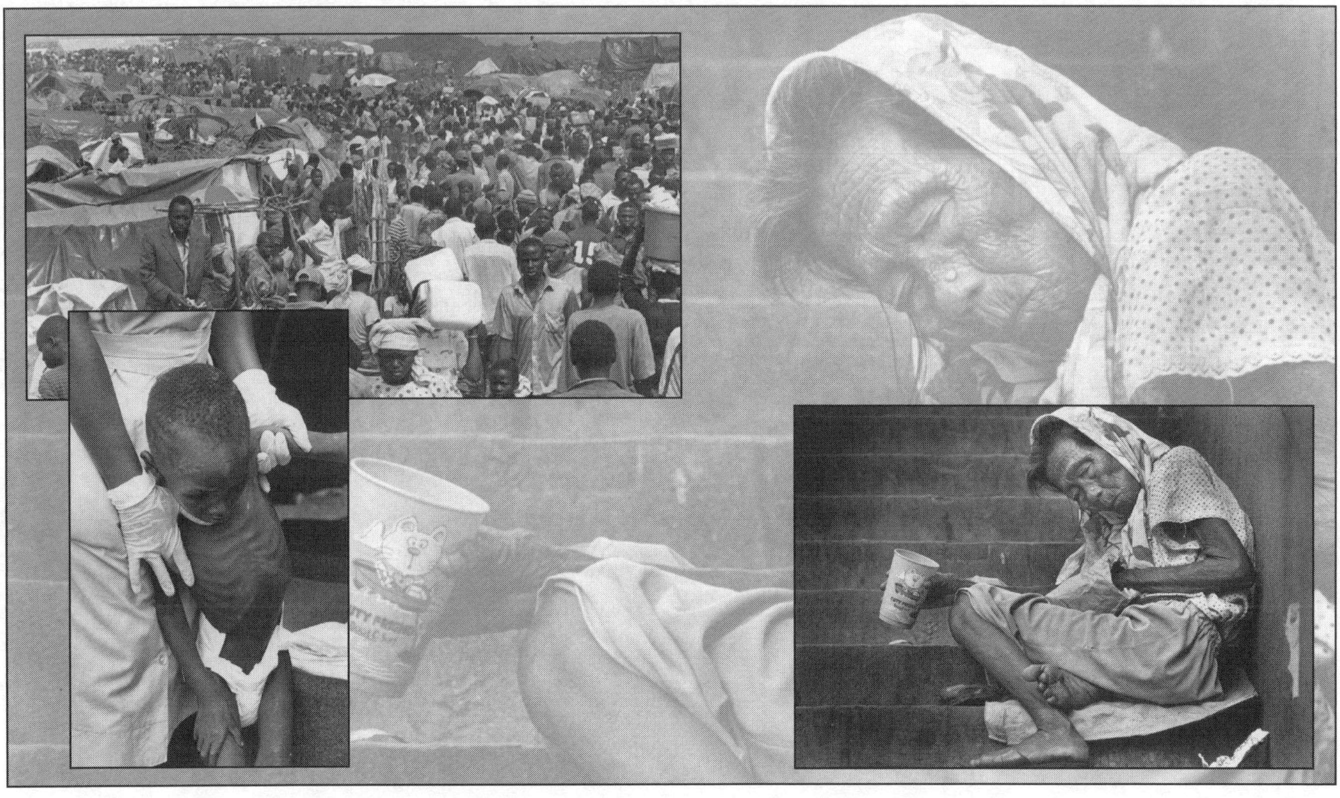

School

Warm-up

- Dictate the following questions – students discuss their answers in groups. What is the best thing about school? The worst? The funniest thing that [has] ever happened to you at school? Your best teacher? Your worst teacher?

Listening

- Play the two pieces without any introduction. Students' task is simply to understand what the speakers are talking about. Get feedback and use this to initiate a conversation on whether students should be divided according to ability or age. If students say age, ask them how they would feel if their English courses were divided according to age rather than level.

1 Well, basically according to age, but, as all Asian countries for cultural reasons, if a child is found to be particularly talented they can actually jump the classes and be admitted into classes two or three classes higher than the one which according to their age they should get into.

2 I think there's something to be said for both sides. I feel that a child who is put in a class according to his ability would always perhaps be younger if if he were a clever boy, would be younger than the rest of the children that he grows up with in the school, and he might lose out especially when he gets to the top of the school there would be perhaps a bigger difference in their age. On the, and if he's kept with his age group I think there's the danger that he would not be extended.

1 Subjects

- Students look at the list of subjects, answer the questions and then discuss their answers in groups.
- As an alternative to the exercise on student's page, brainstorm students on all subjects taught in schools, adding any that students have forgotten. In groups tell them to choose the six most important subjects, rank them, and to add at least two subjects that are not taught in schools that they think would be useful (e.g. memory skills, social skills, newspaper reading, film studies, first aid, environmental and peace studies, plumbing, electrics). In small classes get direct feedback from groups, in larger classes one member of each group should go to another group and explain and discuss his/her group's choices.

2 Teachers

- Give students this information: You are members of the board of governors of a school (real or imaginary). You have to cut down on expenses. Which of the following would you do? **1** Increase the numbers of students per class. **2** Eliminate certain subjects – which ones? **3** Reduce the number of hours spent at school either by reducing the length of the school day or by reducing the number of hours. **4** Sack inefficient teachers – which ones?
- This exercise works well with younger students and even better if they are all from the same school. Encourage them to think about the consequences of their actions but not only in terms of saving money.

Listening

- Students hear two stories (both true!) told by teachers about their lessons. Low level students can simply match the illustration with the anecdotes.

Questions: **1** Why did the first teacher invent an eighth day? What did he call it? **2** What was the purpose of the second teacher's lesson? Why did it go wrong?

1 *To catch those students out who automatically copied everything down. Myday.* **2** *To discuss silence and the reluctance of people to react when they don't know what's going on. Teacher fell asleep.*

1 Actually it was one of the first lessons I'd ever taught, when I first began teaching. I had this beginners class, right, and I'd noticed that everything I wrote down on the blackboard they'd copy down into their books. So we were doing the days of the week, right, and I wrote them all up on the board and I decided to write an eighth day and called it 'My day', and sure enough there were some who diligently wrote it down. I then tried to convince them that in Australia we had eight days a week, but they didn't fall for that one.

2 I've always been interested in psychology and I decided to try out an experiment of my own. I had this advanced class and I wanted to do a lesson on speech and silence. The idea was that I'd go in the class, sit down and say nothing and then see how long it would take for someone in the class to say something. Then the students would be able to compare what they'd been thinking during this silence, plus a general discussion on how silence can be embarrassing, and also why people find it difficult or are reluctant to say something when they don't understand what is going on. The fact is that I fell asleep, this was the last lesson of the day and I hadn't slept much the night before.

- Then, in groups, students discuss the questions on their page. From the results of their answers they should then be able to come up with a definition of an ideal teacher. Get feedback from all the groups and students can then write up a definitive version for homework.

School

1 Subjects

English	geography	psychology	home economics
other foreign language	biology	philosophy	astronomy
your own language	chemistry	religion	arts and crafts
Latin	law	sociology	physical education
literature	mathematics	politics	
history of art	music	economics	
history	physics	computers	

Which of these subjects is the:

- easiest
- most difficult
- most interesting
- most boring
- most useful now
- most needed in the future
- least needed in the future
- one that you'd like to study / have studied but don't/didn't like

2 Teachers

1 What do you learn from your parents that you don't from your teacher? Who do you learn more from?

2 Do you prefer being taught by a male or female teacher? What difference does it make?

3 What is the difference between having a young inexperienced teacher and an old experienced one? Does expert knowledge of a particular subject necessarily imply an ability to teach that subject?

4 Should teachers express their political views in class? Why? Why not?

5 Is the teacher always right? Should you question what the teacher says?

6 Which teacher role is more important – teaching facts, methods and ideas or getting students to learn how to learn?

7 Why is it important for teachers to have a sense of humour?

8 Should teachers call you by your first name or family name? How should you address them?

9 Do you prefer strict teachers or easy-going ones?

10 What do you think a teacher's classroom nightmares are?

11 What subjects are the easiest and most difficult to teach? Why?

12 Are teachers highly respected in your society? Are they paid well?

13 What do you think of this saying? 'Those who can, do, those who can't, teach.'

14 If you were a teacher trainer, what would be the most important things to teach your trainee teachers?

3 Exams

- In groups, students decide whether the statements on their page are true or not. Encourage them to look at the arguments from both points of view, even playing the devil's advocate where necessary.

4 Bright ideas?

- This exercise works best with school children, but is also successful with parents. Tell students that these letters were written by four people taking part in a competition (by the Institute for Social Innovations, Global Ideas Bank) for ideas on how to improve education and parent-child and youth-community relations.
- Divide the class into four groups and assign each group a letter. Their task is to decide how they would put into practice the idea suggested in the letter. Students should be encouraged to extend the ideas as much as possible and to think of all the possible consequences. For example, when discussing community service they should consider when they would do it, for how many hours (and years), what kind of services are needed and what they could offer, what would be the benefits not only to the community but also to the participants themselves, etc.
- Rearrange the groups so that there is at least one member of each project in each new group. Students now explain to each other what their original group decided. They then vote on the best idea. Finally, get class feedback and decide as a whole class what the most interesting, practical or useful idea was.
- Put students into pairs and ask them to act out one of these role-plays. Choose a good pair and ask them to act out their piece in front of the class.
  (a) Child telling parent that he/she's failed an exam.
  (b) Child telling parent that he/she wants to leave school and get a job.
  (c) Parent telling child that he/she (the child) must leave school and get a job.
  (d) Headteacher telling another teacher that his/her teaching is not up to standard.
  (e) A teacher/professor telling student that they might as well stop studying as they have no chance of progress.
  (f) Teacher telling parent that child has been bullying another child.
  (g) Parent complaining to teacher that he/she has been victimising their child.

3 Exams

1 Exams are the most effective way to test a student's knowledge and ability.

2 The best way to study for an exam is to do it with a fellow student.

3 When preparing for an exam it is better to study a few points in depth, than everything superficially.

4 Rather than studying for hours on end, it is better to study in hourly blocks interspersed with short breaks.

5 It is impossible to study efficiently with background music playing.

6 The time spent preparing for exams would be better spent learning new things.

7 There is no point studying the night before the exam.

8 Nerves help you to perform better in exams.

9 Dictionaries and calculators should not be allowed to be used in exams.

10 Exam time is worse for students than for teachers.

4 Bright ideas?

a

My schoolmates and I have been doing community service for nearly a year now, and we just wanted to share with you some of our experiences. We all know that this town is a complete mess – no places for us to go, beggars in the streets, old people lonely at home, vandalism, graffiti and litter everywhere ...

b

I'm 16 and two weeks ago I signed a contract with my parents on how they want me to behave and what I expect from them in return. Already my relationship with them has really got better, and I'd recommend it for all teenagers like myself who have difficulty getting on with ...

c

While I was on holiday in America last summer I watched an amazing TV programme. There was a DJ and four or five teachers and you could ring in and ask them questions about your homework. Apparently in the first week they got more than 20,000 callers. Why don't we ...

d

Our school has just begun a wonderful new project. Instead of teachers doing all the teaching, we teach each other for a few hours a week. At the moment we're just doing this within one class, but we're thinking of getting older children to teach younger children, and maybe even ...

Time

Warm-ups

- Dictate the following activities to students: food preparation, eating, dishwashing, housekeeping, shopping, school/paid work, studying at home, travelling, physical exercise, meeting friends/going out, watching TV, reading/hobbies, personal care/hygiene, sleeping (and any others they can think of). Students then have to write down how much time (in hours) in a week they spend doing them. When they have written the number of hours for each item, tell them to total them up and see how accurately they accounted for their time (there are 168 hours in a week). They can then make any adjustments they want.

- In pairs, they now ask each other questions, e.g. How much time do you spend doing x? How many hours do you ...? Do you spend as much time doing x as you do y? What do you spend the most/least time on? What would you like to spend less time on? When you were younger did you use to spend more or less time on x?

- Do times vary between men and women? If so, why? How does this compare with how students used to spend their time say 5/10/15 years ago? How does this compare with their parents' generation? Has the proportion of time we spend doing certain things changed much over the past 15 years? How will it change in the future? (e.g. less work more leisure, more time saving devices).

1 Clocking out

- Students read the text and then discuss questions in groups.

2 Tomorrow

- While reading the text, students should underline what they consider to be the three most and three least important future developments. They should then discuss these in their group.

Writing

- 'It is one of our few possessions in life, that we cannot foretell the future' (Ivy Compton Burnett). Discuss.

Time

1 Clocking out

We tend to forget that we didn't always have clocks. The majority of people's days were regulated by the cock crowing and the sun setting. It was only really during the Industrial Revolution, when factory workers' hours needed to be checked, that clocks really became an essential item. With the advent of the railway too, accuracy in time-keeping was more necessary.

1 What would life be like if we didn't have clocks? Would there be any advantages?

2 In what areas of life is an accurate clock or watch crucially important?

3 What would be the consequences of the whole world being at the same time (e.g. it would be 12 o'clock in London, New York and Sydney simultaneously)?

4 How many hours do you think should be in the working/school day and week?

5 Do you ever feel that you would like to step out of time? Why, and what would you do?

2 Tomorrow

WHAT IS TOMORROW GOING TO BE?

Who can tell what inventions, new dimensions, and revolutionary ways of life will come into being? Free travel to other planets? No money, or money in a different form? One government all over the world?

▶ Perhaps new sounds and colours will appear. We may be able to enter the fifth, sixth, and seventh dimensions. We will converse intelligently with all the animals on earth.

▶ We may find contact with other times, and be able to communicate with the dead. The future and the past will be open books to us.

▶ We may be able to create new life at will, without the bother of conceiving and giving birth. We might have more control over our own bodies, and grow new limbs and organs as we need them.

▶ There will no longer be banks and taxes and fines; there will be much more sophisticated ways of doing things. The police will have gone to some other world.

▶ Thought will be all-powerful, and will be the instrument of all these changes.

▶ People will exist in several versions, eliminating jealousy. Attractive men and women will be made in hundreds of editions.

▶ There may no longer be limitations on time and space, so no one need ever again be late. Geniuses will no longer be needed; everyone can think himself a genius and it will be so.

▶ The means at our disposal will be unlimited and nothing need ever again be impossible.

3 Are you a victim of time?

- Students brainstorm fictional (or factual) attempts at beating time and space, e.g. H.G. Wells' *Time machine*, the films *Back To The Future*, *Dr Who*, *Total Recall*, *Star Trek*. Students discuss whether it will ever be possible to move back and forward in time. Alternatively students discuss films or literature which attempt to recreate a period of history or a time in the future. What are the implications for the production teams making the film? What do they have to take into consideration when recreating the period? How important is it to get the details right?
- Students now read the short passage and answer the questions. Then in groups they decide which questions are aimed at discovering whether someone lives (a) in the past (b) in the present (c) in the future.
- Students analyse each others' answers and should imagine that they are psychologists who have to give their 'patients' advice on their relationship with time.

past: *1, 3, 6, 9a* **present:** *5, 7, 8a, 8b, 9b* **future:** *2, 4, 8c, 9c*

4 How long? How old?

- Ask students to read all the questions and add any more they wish to add. They then turn over their photocopy, and in pairs ask each other the questions that they remember.

Listening

- Students hear some people's answers to the questions on student's page. Students' task is first to identify the question, and then to write down the time or age.

1 *a (half an hour)* **2** *e (forever)* **3** *g (7 years old)* **4** *e (impossible)* **5** *a (20 minutes)* **6** *g (10 years old)* **7** *h (16 years old)* **8** *k (snow – ten)* **9** *a (thirty minutes or a quarter of an hour)*

1 It depends really what time I went to bed the night before, but probably about half an hour, just enough time to have a quick cup of coffee and then off to work.

2 Takes me forever actually. I can't understand them at all. And, my mother always asks me to to do them for her, but I am no better than she is really.

3 I remember that very clearly. I was about seven. And I remember spending the whole morning sitting on my bicycle completely stationary, trying to balance and not fall off.

4 I can't understand instruction manuals, no matter how many times I try and read them they are absolutely impossible, especially ones for video recorders.

5 It takes me about 20 minutes to get ready to go to work.

6 I learned how to ride a bike, this is embarrassing to say, when I was about ten years old, and the rest of my family and all my friends used to ridicule me. And that's probably why it took me so long. It also took me about the same amount of time to learn to swim.

7 The first time I went on holiday without my family was when I was 16 and I went on a tour of the world on a bicycle.

8 There's not a great deal of snow in South Africa. And I think I first saw it when I was about ten.

9 If I have a bath when I get up, I think I'm bathed and dressed in half an hour. If I don't have a bath I should say I'm dressed and washed in ten minutes to quarter of an hour.

3 Are you a victim of time?

Where do you stand in the passage of time?

Do you want to spend so much time saving it that you then don't know what to do with it? Are you constantly planning for tomorrow or are you mournfully looking back into the past? Try this test and find out.

1 Do you spend a lot of time saying 'if only' or 'I wish'?

2 Do you believe that change is not only inevitable but highly desirable?

3 If they sold tickets to the past would you go there?

4 Have you ever had your hand read by a fortune-teller?

5 Would you like to wake up one morning with no memory of the past?

6 Do you keep a diary and regularly look at old photos?

7 Does the thought that the world might end tomorrow excite you at all?

8 If you won a million dollars would you
(a) spend the lot?
(b) buy a cottage in the country?
(c) invest it in stocks and shares?

9 Which of the following would you choose as your motto?
(a) Those who do not remember the past are condemned to relive it (George Santayana).
(b) Gather ye rosebuds while ye may (Robert Herrick).
(c) Forgetting those things which are behind, and reaching forth unto those things which are before, this is wisdom (*The Bible*, Philippians 3:13).

4 How long? How old?

How long does it take you to do the following activities?

a Get up and get dressed in the morning.

b Get to school or work.

c Have lunch.

d Read one page of a novel in your own language. And in English?

e Understand instructions in manuals.

f Understand jokes in your own language. And in English?

How old were you when you first did the following?

g Learned how to ride a bike.

h Went on a holiday without your family.

i Had a dream in English.

j Earned some money.

k Saw the sea/snow/mountains.

l Cooked yourself or someone else a meal.

Unusual

Warm-up

- Dictate the following questions (or alternatively get students to invent their own questions):
  1 What's the most unusual experience you've ever had?
  2 Who's the most unusual person you've ever met?
  3 Where's the most unusual place you've ever been?
  4 What's the most unusual thing you've ever bought?
  5 What's the most unusual thing you've ever been given?
  6 What's the most unusual film you've ever seen?
  7 What's the most unusual book you've ever read?
  8 What's the most unusual sight you've ever seen?
  9 Who has the most unusual face you've ever seen?
  10 Who's the most unusual teacher you've ever had?

- Students then have to write the answers to at least three of the questions, without writing the number of the question. They then show their answers to their partner who has to match them with the questions. Finally, they discuss their answers.

1 Coincidences?

- Students read the text and discuss the answers in groups. Then ask students to come up with a rational explanation for the coincidence surrounding twins separated at birth. They can then check their ideas with the listening exercise.

Listening

- Students hear some rational explanations for the similarities between the identical twins mentioned in the text.
  Questions: 1 What is the logical explanation for the twins **(a)** having seven rings? **(b)** getting married on the same day? **2** What do these coincidences imply?

1a *rich husbands able to afford to buy them rings, slender hands so they'd want to show rings off, superstition, coincidence* **1b** *High statistical chance (actually 1 in 125)* **2** *Our personality and lifestyle is not only controlled by the environment but is also determined by our genes.*

A So what's the big deal?

B The fact that they both had seven rings doesn't strike you as being a bit strange?

A OK. So they both had rich husbands who could afford the rings and presumably they'd both got nice slender hands which they'd obviously want to show off, and anyway, you could say it was just chance that they both had seven; seven's supposed to be a lucky number anyway, and they both might have been superstitious. You know there could be hundreds of reasons to explain that. I mean me and my best friend, we both wear two rings on our little finger, always have done, it doesn't prove anything.

B What about the watch and the bracelets?

A More coincidences.

B Right. Well what about them getting married on the same day?

A Actually there's not much strange about that either. I seem to remember that when we did statistics at high school the teacher told us that the chances of getting married on the same day were about one in a hundred. You forget that most people get married on a Saturday, some months are more popular than others, and people tend to get married at a similar age anyway.

B But the same dress? Same flowers?

A Listen Al. What are you driving at? We're talking about genetics here, not about the supernatural. And anyway let's suppose it's not coincidence, then what?

B Well it has enormous implications. The fact that these twins were separated at birth and brought up in two different parts of the country by different parents, shows that it really is genetics, that our life may not only be controlled by the environment, but by what we inherit from our parents.

A But did you really need some whizz-kid psychologists to tell you that? I mean, what can I say? Yes, you're right. But we already knew that, didn't we?

Here are some more explanations that are not mentioned in the listening. Some similarities between separated twins may be explained in terms of physiology. Because they share all their genes, identical twins are likely to develop the same hereditary illnesses. Medical problems can affect other aspects of life – financial, occupational, social and educational. Similarities in the economic and social conditions of life may also lead to specific similarities in behaviour. For example, people in the US who have modest incomes may be more likely to vacation in Florida, where a holiday is relatively inexpensive.

2 Cults?

- Students read all the cases (all based on fact).
- In groups they then answer the questions. Get class feedback on which case seems to be the most unusual.

Unusual

1 Coincidences?

One of the best known collection of parallels is between the careers of Abraham Lincoln and John F Kennedy; both were shot while sitting next to their wives; both were succeeded by a Southerner named Johnson; both their killers were themselves killed before they could be brought to justice. Lincoln had a secretary called Kennedy; Kennedy a secretary called Lincoln. Lincoln was killed in the Ford Theatre; Kennedy was killed in a Ford Lincoln – and so on.

Similar connections are found between identical twins who have been separated at birth. Dorothy Lowe and Bridget Harrison were separated in 1945, and did not meet until 1979, when they were flown over from Britain for an investigation by Dr Tom Bouchard, a psychologist at the University of Minnesota. They found that when they met they were both wearing seven rings on their hands, two bracelets on one wrist, a watch and a bracelet on the other. They married on the same day, had worn identical wedding dresses and carried the same flowers. Dorothy had named her son Richard Andrew, and her daughter, Catherine Louise; Bridget had named her son Andrew Richard and her daughter Karen Louise (she had wanted to call her Catherine). Both had a cat called Tiger. Dorothy loved the historical novels of Catherine Cookson; Bridget loved the historical novels of Caroline Merchant (Catherine Cookson's other pen name). They had a string of similar mannerisms when nervous ...

a Are the situations outlined in the text coincidences or something else? Can you think of any rational explanations for these facts?

b What are the implications of the fact that these identical twins had so many things in common? Is what we inherit from our parents stronger than how we are conditioned by our environment?

c Have you ever had the feeling that it's a small world when you've met someone you know thousands of kilometres away from home, or in some unusual circumstances?

d What has been the biggest coincidence in your life so far?

2 Cults

1 This man claims that the cells in his body have switched their DNA programming from death to life. Many people, especially the elderly, have paid him considerable sums of money to obtain his secret of eternal life.

2 On several occasions this man has assembled members of his congregation to hill tops to await the end of the world. On previous occasions some of the more fanatical members killed both themselves and members of their family before the terrible event, as they believed that they would be able to get to heaven quicker than the others.

3 This man claims he is the Messiah. He has founded a cult group and barricaded himself and his members into a heavily armed fortress. He expects all kinds of favours from his members, all of whom have been brainwashed into worshipping him.

4 This organisation freezes its 'patients' immediately after clinical death in the hope that science will find a way to revitalize such people in the future and rejuvenate their bodies. The patients pay around $150,000 for this privilege.

1 Which of the four cases (all based on fact) seems the most unusual to you?

2 Would you become a member of any of these cult/organisations? Why do people join such cults and why do they believe their leaders?

3 Do you think any of them should be taken to court for fraudulent behaviour? If so, what sentence should they be given?

4 Supposing what these people claim is true – what would the consequences be?

3 Unusualtopia

Only for on-the-ball and off-the-wall students (and teachers!).

- Inform students that a group of people have created their own mini-Utopia which has now been successfully operating for 100 years. In groups, students have to discuss the rationale behind, and the implications of, the ten statements about the utopia, i.e. why the inhabitants decided to instigate these ideas and what the consequences are, and whether they themselves agree with the ideas.
- Now proceed either with the listening exercise (below) or ask students to match the statements with the four extracts (**A–D**) from *The Partially Correct Guide to a Better Planet*. The extracts can then be discussed in groups.

A *f* **B** *e* **C** *j* **D** *a*

Listening

- Students listen to extracts from a discussion with members of the unusualtopia. Their task is firstly to identify which statement(s) is/are being discussed (**NB** extracts may refer to more than one question), and secondly the reasons for the policy in question.
- After listening students discuss some of what they've heard and discuss whether they would like to live in this Utopia or not.

1 *f* **2** *e* **3** *i, j* **4** *b, c, g*

1 Well actually there's a very good reason for that. The first six years are spent in play groups, then the kids are ready to begin working. We don't actually call it working, but learning. They watch people doing things, like a cook making a cake, a mechanic mending a car. They help where they can and constantly gain experience. By the time they're 14 they're ready to begin really working. This stops when they're around 30 and it's only at this point that school begins. Our view is that you can't learn anything unless you experience it and nor can you teach anything you haven't experienced directly yourself. So there are no teachers as such, just exchanges of information and practical demonstrations by people who've generated their own particular interests and wish to communicate them to others.

2 Yes but this doesn't mean that there is no reward for working hard. You are actually paid more in time rather than money. If you think about it, you can't actually do much with constantly increasing amounts of money, it's far more sensible to have more time which you can use really beneficially. The result is that everyone works hard because no one wants to spend all their life in an office, factory or whatever.

3 Our philosophy is that people should be totally independent. Any kind of health service makes people dependent on it. Living with the same people the whole time may mean that you get into bad habits, you may become emotionally dependent, you may lose your vitality and routines can become very stultifying. Change is an exhilarating experience, it means progress both at a national and personal level. People also depend on their possessions, become obsessed by having more and more. If, on the other hand, you have very few, as we have here, you lose this dependence and as a consequence need no external authority, like a police force, to protect your possessions.

4 These are obviously all for environmental reasons. We've virtually eliminated air pollution, everything's solar powered, there are no traffic jams, no ugly exterior architecture and no need for paper.

3 Unusualtopia

a Women speak one language, men another.

b Buildings are all built underground.

c There is no private transport.

d All governmental decisions are taken by a computer.

e Everyone is paid the same salary.

f There are no teachers in schools.

g All books and newspapers are in disk format.

h Everyone writes down the dreams they have at night.

i No-one above the age of 18 can live with the same person/people for more than five years.

j There are no doctors and no police force.

A

What is the best age to go to school? We generally study non-scientific subjects (i.e. not physics, maths, etc.) at a point in our lives when we are possibly least able to understand what it is we are learning. This is particularly true of literature, philosophy, psychology, and sociology, where we may be ill-equipped to understand the full meaning of these subjects, as they very much depend on our own experiences. However, if we had the opportunity to really live before we actually studied these subjects, then we would be able to appreciate them much more. One might of course argue that not having experience of something doesn't necessarily mean that you can't learn or teach it – the fact that priests, etc. can tell us how to run our love lives is a good example of this.

B

Money is supposedly the prime motivating factor in the world of work, but an ever-increasing salary is no guarantee that a person will work harder and more efficiently, nor that they will be any happier. The advantage of being 'paid' in time rather than money, is that you are far more motivated to do things quickly (as Parkinson's law states: the time it takes you to do something expands to the time you have available). Speed, of course, doesn't necessarily mean efficiency, and checks would obviously need to be made on how well the job is being done.

C

If there were no health service people would be much more conscious of looking after themselves – they would do more physical exercise, stop smoking and drinking, etc. – because they would know that they could not fall back on a free service if they did get ill through their own excesses. Of course, some illnesses are not always the responsibility of the person who has them. Provisions would have to be taken for such people.

D

The current trend towards levelling and making everyone feel that they are basically the same is leading to a dull society which is frightened of acknowledging that in fact we are all different. What we are now getting is a mono-culture of burgers and cola, moving towards one language and one currency, with an educational cleansing process which sees diversity as somehow shameful. So-called 'World Music' is bracketing together so many cultures and diluting their music with western technology and ideas, that in the end an Indian sitar player will be indistinguishable from a Turkish oud player or a Cockney guitar player. The fact that in our utopia men and women speak different languages is a symbolic gesture to highlight that we are different and that we are proud of it. Women and men are built differently, and often think and talk differently too. Of course, we do have a common language, but our philosophy is *equal but different.*

Vision

Warm-up

- Tell students to study the picture at the top of their page for 30 seconds. Divide the class into groups of two or three. Looking at the picture, student 1 interrogates students 2 and 3 (who have their picture covered) to see how accurately they remember the details.
- At the end of the lesson or at the beginning of the next, ask students to look at the picture on the other page (they must have the first picture covered). Students should then write down any differences they find. The scenes are in fact identical.
  Psychologists have shown that if you give people a task then they are motivated to try and do it. Since they assume that the task can be done, they will try and produce some result, i.e. in this case they will think they have found some differences.

1 Could you be an eyewitness?

- Students read the passage.

Writing

- Divide class into two. Group 1 leaves while Group 2 watches a video of an accident or bank robbery (or whatever you can get hold of). Group 2 returns to watch the same video (though you tell them it's a different one), while Group 1 leaves the room. For homework, ask students to write a reasonably detailed description of what happened. Next lesson, pair a student from Group 1 with one from Group 2. They should then read each other's description under the guise of correcting the English. See how many students discover that they have watched the same video!

2 Talking blindly

- Before looking at the student's page, brainstorm the subject of blindness. What things can/could students do with their eyes closed? How many famous blind people can they think of? To simulate a real life experience, in pairs S1 could lead a blindfolded S2 around the classroom. S2 then describes his/her sensations.
- Students now look at the list on their page and, in groups, decide which of these activities blind people might have problems with, and what solutions have been found or could be found to help the blind in these activities.

Listening

- Ask students to look at the illustrations of braille writing. Ask them if they know what it is and who invented it. Students then listen and answer these questions. Low level students simply put the illustrations in order while they listen.
  Questions: **1** Was Louis Braille born blind? **2** In what year did Braille go to a school for the blind? **3** How big were the letters in the reading books? **4** What was 'night writing'? **5** Was Braille's system only used for reading words?

Order of illustrations: *c, a, d, b*

1 *no* **2** *1818* **3** *7cm by 5cm* **4** *a means for letting soldiers communicate in the dark* **5** *no, for music too*

Louis Braille was only four years old when he lost his sight as a result of an accident. Yet he turned his personal tragedy into a great and lasting triumph. In 1818, at the age of 10 he went to a school for the blind in Paris, where he learnt the alphabet by running his fingers along big letters formed by pieces of wood. He then learned to read by feeling his way over enlarged words in special books. Each letter was about 7 cm high and 5 cm wide, so not only were the books very big but they also took a long time to read. So Louis set out to devise a compact code with raised symbols for words and phrases. He tried various codes based on squares, circles and triangles cut out of leather. He then heard of a new system of 'night writing' that would enable soldiers in the field to communicate with each other during darkness. This system consisted of a series of raised dots and dashes punched into strips of cardboard that could be read by touch without using a light. This became the basis of Braille's system which he revised and perfected, including even musical notations, until death at the early age of 42 in 1852.

Vision

1 Could you be an eyewitness?

Eyewitnesses to the assassination of Senator Robert Kennedy in 1968, claimed that he had been shot at at a distance of between one to three meters. Yet the autopsy showed that the gun must have been virtually touching his head.

What we remember as eyewitnesses can easily be distorted by how we are interrogated by the police. A question phrased like 'How fast were the cars going when they crashed into each other?' is more likely to get an overestimation of speed than if 'contacted' had been used instead of 'crashed into'. In other cases just using the definite rather than the indefinite article, can have a significant effect on your answer. If you are asked, for example, 'did you see the man with the gun?' you are far more likely to 'remember' having seen a gun (even if there wasn't one) than if you were asked 'did you see a man with a gun?'.

2 Talking blindly

reading
walking
listening
talking
sports
cooking
having children
art and music
finding a job
appreciating nature
make-up and personal appearance
falling in love
everyday human relationships
using public transport
typing
choosing clothes
driving
being accepted by other people

a

b

c

d

3 Points of view

This is the kind of exercise that only works with on-the-ball sensitive students.

- Students read Henry Ford's (founder of the Ford Motor Company, and famous for saying 'History is bunk.') quotation. Make sure they understand the meaning, and why it is important to understand other people's points of view.
- Ask students to read the eleven situations. In pairs, their task is to choose two or three of the situations. They should then analyse these situations from the various viewpoints and decide who is in the most difficult position. Finally, they choose one situation and improvise a dialogue between two of the people in that situation.
- Now choose some pairs to act out their dialogue in front of the class. The rest of the class has to identify which situation is being acted out.

Writing

- Students imagine they were a third person who observed but didn't participate in the above dialogues. Their task is to write down this third person's viewpoint of what happened, quoting either in direct or indirect speech from what the two people said, adding their own observations and then reaching some kind of conclusion.

4 Optical illusions

- Students first match the descriptions with the illusions. Then, in groups students look at the optical illusions and should try and explain them to students in their group who don't understand them.

1 *b* **2** *c* **3** *d* **4** *a*

Extra

- Put some objects in a plastic bag. Either by feeling the shape from outside, or putting their hand inside but without looking, students have to guess what they are. As a result of this experience students should decide which of these two senses, sight and touch, is the most developed, and when touch may be more important than sight.

Vision

3 Points of view

'If there is any one secret of success, it lies in the ability to get the other person's point of view and see things from that person's angle as well as from your own.' (Henry Ford)

1 Person looking at a mother smacking a child in the street.

2 School children listening to their teacher telling off one of their classmates.

3 Father seeing his daughter kissing with her boyfriend who is of a different race and colour.

4 Child listening to his/her parents shouting at each other.

5 Old couple looking at a youth with brightly coloured hair.

6 Emaciated African child looking at overweight Western couple.

7 Someone watching a store detective catching an obviously poor woman stealing food.

8 Nurse at a cosmetic surgeon's waiting room making an appointment for a disfigured child and a beautiful woman with a slightly bent nose.

9 Son presenting his considerably older fiancée to his mother and father.

10 Someone watching a woman reversing her car into a parked car with a man inside.

4 Optical illusions

a

b

c

d

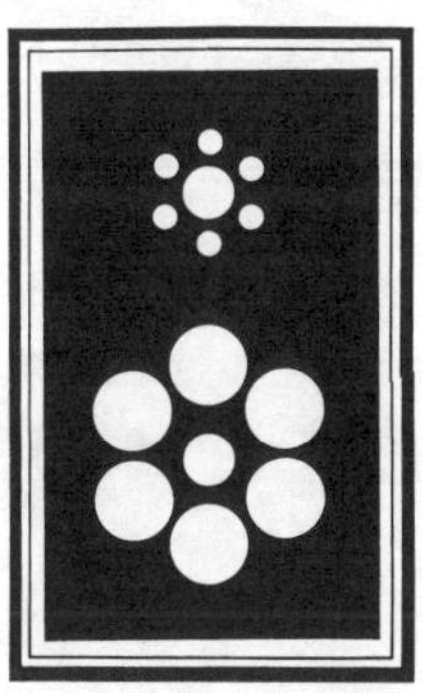

1 What do you see in the middle of the frame? Is it a letter B or is it the number 13? It depends on which you saw first – the horizontal ABC or the vertical 12, 13, 14.

2 What is your first impression – a rabbit or a duck.

3 The centre petal on the flower below looks smaller than the one above - yet they are both the same.

4 Very slowly read the words in the hat – what does it say?

Wants

Warm-ups

- Students discuss what they would like to change in themselves from all points of view – physically, psychologically, in love, in work, at school, things they wish they were better at, etc. They should discuss with their partners how likely they are to achieve them. This activity leads directly into **1 Wishes**.

- Students discuss things they would like to change in others – this could be in members of the class, in you the teacher, in their family, friends etc.

1 Wishes

- Ask students to read all the wishes and select the five things they would wish for most. They should assume that there are no strings attached and that what they wish for will turn out to be just as they wanted. In small groups they then discuss these wishes.
- Now explain that this exercise is based on a test (from *Sex roles* Vol. 26 May 1991) performed by psychologists on college students to find out if men's and women's desires are different. In the original test there were 48 wishes and subjects had to choose their top ten. The list on the student's page begins with the most popular wishes (i.e. of the psychologists' subjects) going down to the least popular. In their groups students identify what the typical female wishes would be and what conclusions can be drawn from this.

ⓘ Females outweighed males in desiring wishes **1, 2, 5** and **7** to come true, and had an equal desire for **15** and **16**. The conclusions of the psychologists were that the wishes more favoured by the women tend to be those generally preferred by both genders. In addition, they tend to be concerned with 'real life' issues involving other people. In sharp contrast men's wishes seem to involve the desire to be free of reality constraints, and seem to be relatively impersonal.

Writing

- 'It is better to have than wish.' Discuss.

2 Regrets

Ask students to look at the questions. They might find it embarrassing to talk about their regrets; though the listening exercise should indicate to them that the regrets could be quite banal and don't have to be overly personal.

Listening

- Students hear some people talking about the major regrets in their lives. Their task is simply to note down what the regrets are.
- Play the first three pieces to give students an idea of the kind of regrets that can be revealed without embarrassment. Elicit the relevant constructions (I wish, if only). With the right kind of group you could also play the fourth and fifth pieces, which are more personal. Students can then move on to discussing their own regrets and the other questions on their page.

1 *restarting smoking* **2** *not learning the piano* **3** *being angry with someone* **4** *not having really known her brothers* **5** *everything up to the age of 30*

1 My biggest regret was starting smoking again. I gave up for about two years and then I went to a wedding and somebody, a girl I hadn't seen for a few years, was there smoking, and I thought oh it'll be all right to have one. So I had one of her cigarettes and I really wish I hadn't.

2 My biggest regret was not learning the piano. I had a couple of lessons when I was quite young and I wish I hadn't given them up, basically.

3 If I do have a regret, I often wish I hadn't spoken to somebody the way I had, because I was in a bad mood, or if only I'd been a bit more polite and things like that.

4 My biggest regret is not knowing my brothers very well. We went to different schools and even if we lived in the same house we only ever saw each other for holidays. And when I left home to go to university I realised that I was living with two people I didn't know.

5 I regret pretty much everything I did until I was 30. I chose the wrong university, fell in love with all the wrong people, got married far too young. Then I bought a house, opened a school and had a child all in one year. I just wish I wasn't so impulsive and that I could learn to do one thing at a time.

Writing

- (a) Students imagine and write down what regrets they think their parents or other members of family have. This could be extended to friends or even famous people. (b) Regret is a stronger emotion than pleasure. Discuss (for philosophers only!).

Wants

1 Wishes

1 To deeply love a person who deeply loves me.

2 For there to be peace on earth, and no more war.

3 To have the talent and ability to succeed at anything I choose.

4 To be recognised as the best at something.

5 For there to be a clean environment, free from pollution.

6 To be able to travel in time.

7 To be very attractive.

8 To understand the meaning of life.

9 To be youthful all my life.

10 To be able to read people's minds.

11 To be able to be invisible.

12 To live as long as I want.

13 To have a lot of children.

14 To be able to take revenge on my enemies.

15 To be able to change appearance, age, sex and race whenever I want.

16 To be reincarnated with all my memories.

2 Regrets

'Regrets I have a few, but then again too few to mention.'

1 If your life were on a videotape and you could go back and edit parts out, what parts would you change?

2 Is there anyone's advice which you regret having or not having taken?

3 Is there anyone who you wish you had never met? Which person from your past would you most like to see again?

4 Yeats, the Irish poet, wrote:

One looks back to one's youth as to a cup that a madman, dying of thirst, left half-tasted.

Will this be the case when you are old (i.e. that you will feel that you didn't take all the opportunities that you should have done)? Are you satisfied with your life? Do you feel you have (and need to have) a purpose? Do you set yourself goals? Do you think you make good use of your time?

3 Wants

- Before beginning the exercise, students discuss what people basically want from life. They can then compare their wants with Dale Carnegie's. They should now put Carnegie's wants in their own order of importance and then compare and justify their choices. If you think 'sexual gratification' would cause embarrassment simply white it out before you do the photocopies.
- Students now answer the questions.

Writing

- Students write down a few examples from their answers to questions **1** and **5**, e.g. I wish I didn't have to ..., They wanted me to ...

ⓘ (4) 'I want doesn't get' is a typical parent's reply to a child who says 'I want an ice-cream.' rather than 'Can I have an ice-cream?' However, the idea here is to discuss those things that children wish for but parents refuse to buy (e.g. I wanted my parents to get me a metal detector, they refused so I sold a gold coin I had and bought one. I then found a cache of Roman coins and two swords!).

(8) Students may have some trouble understanding this one. It could be a wonderful philosophy for life. Basically, rather than trying to get what you want (you'll always want more in any case), you should enjoy and appreciate the things you already have and future things you may get. But it does not mean blind and resigned acceptance of your situation.

4 Waste not want not

- Ask students to guess how much rubbish their family produces every year. Then get them to refer to the bin statistics on their page. They can also see Britain's record of dumping waste into the North Sea and Irish Sea. These statistics relate to the early 1990s and have been considerably rounded; the situation has improved a little since then.
- Now students do the quiz in pairs. They should decide whether their partner is a waster or not. **NB** Point out that 'waster' also means a 'good for nothing person'.

ⓘ Recycling also saves considerably on air and water pollution. For instance, producing steel from scrap reduces air pollution by 85% and water pollution by 76%; for recycling paper, the reductions are 74% for air pollution and 35% for water pollution.

3 Wants

Dale Carnegie in his 30 million copy selling book *How to win friends and influence people* identified eight principle wants:

a feeling of importance

food

health and the preservation of life

life in the hereafter

money and the things money will buy

sleep

the well-being of our children

sexual gratification

1 What do you do that you don't want to do?

2 Do you do things that you don't want to do only because you feel you are expected to do them by other people, or to fit in with their wishes?

3 What things did you want to do when you were younger that you don't want to do now, and vice versa?

4 'I want doesn't get.' What things did you want as a child that your parents refused to get you or allow you to do?

5 What things did your parents want for you? And what do you want for your children?

6 If you really want to do something you can do it. True or false?

7 If everybody in the world could have what they wanted would the world be a better place?

8 Is it better to get what you want or want what you get?

4 Waste not want not

are you a waster?

- I generally leave the water running while brushing my teeth.
- I usually divide my rubbish up into bottles, paper, etc.
- Whenever I can I try to buy glass rather than plastic bottles.
- I often take the car when I could walk or go by bus.
- I never forget to turn the light off when I'm not in the room.
- When I'm not watching TV it's always on stand-by.
- I avoid making photocopies where possible.
- I always leave a clean plate at meal times.
- I rarely take a bath, but nearly always take a shower.
- I hardly ever remember to take my own bag to the supermarket.

Xenophobia

Warm-up

- Elicit adjectives which describe personality. When you have a fairly long list, ask students to try and associate a nationality with the characteristics. Alternatively, write the names of a few countries on the board and get students to suggest characteristics which they associate with people from these countries. They then read out the characteristics and the others have to guess which nationality they refer to.

1 The English

NB This extract comes from a book by an English person satirising the English way of life. It is by no means intended as a serious piece, nor does it necessarily reflect the views of the majority of English.

- Introduce this exercise by asking students, in groups, to invent a quiz entitled 'Are you a typical English person?' (you can obviously vary the title to suit the nationality). Students then change groups and ask each other their questions and decide on the most 'English' person in the class. You may like to point out that English is not the same as British, which also includes Welsh, Scots and Northern Irish.
- Students then read the text and discuss questions.

ⓘ 'fastness' = security

2 Apartheid

This exercise might be rather sensitive for some students, particularly in mixed black and white classes. The exercise may promote little discussion, but I hope this will be compensated for by a little soul searching.

- Brainstorm students on the meaning of apartheid (literally 'apartness', segregation of whites, Africans, Coloureds and Indians) and the injustices that blacks suffered. Students now read the text and then do the listening.

Listening

- Students hear a white South African (of English origin now living outside South Africa, but has a Zulu daughter-in-law who is a member of parliament) talking about what blacks couldn't do in South Africa before the elections in 1994. The students' task is to write down what these things are (many of which were mentioned in the text). Pre-teach the vocabulary relating to building houses.

They weren't allowed the same jobs as whites.
They weren't allowed to build houses.
They had to use separate entrances in post offices.
They couldn't eat in white restaurants.
They weren't allowed to sit with white people in parks, bus stops, etc.
They couldn't go to white cinemas or use white public transport.

In South Africa before the elections well, and even now, the whites have had everything going for them. They've had, been able to have good jobs, and lots of servants and they've lived very well. Because before apartheid was done away with, blacks were not allowed to hold down jobs that whites could have; they were, the government didn't want them to have a good education so that they were able to take on jobs. Even they were not even allowed to build houses; they could mix the cement and hand the bricks to a white builder, but they were to allowed to build, to lay the bricks. Well there were separate entrances for white people and black people in post offices, and ... quite often in restaurants of course they were never allowed into a white restaurant, but they, some in some they could go round to the back and be served from the kitchen. There were special benches for white people in parks and at bus-stops, the blacks were not allowed to travel on white buses or in white trains. They were not allowed to go to cinemas, the white cinemas.

Xenophobia

Xenophobia is the English national sport – England's most enduring cultural expression. And there is a very good reason for that.

As far as the English are concerned, all of life's greatest problems can be summed up in one word – foreigners.

Nine hundred years ago the last invasion of England was perpetrated by the Normans. They settled, tried to integrate themselves with the indigenous population and failed.

The indigenous population then, as now, displayed an utter contempt for them not merely because they had conquered but more importantly because they had come from abroad.

The English don't just believe themselves superior to all other nations. They also believe that all other nations secretly know that they are.

They feel themselves to be natural leaders, the most obvious choice for 'top nation'. Geography reinforces this belief as the inhabitants look out to the sea all around them from the fastness of their 'tight little island'. Nobody would ever question the aptness of the newspaper report: 'Fog in the Channel – Continent cut off.'

1 The English

1 Do you think this extract is serious or humorous? Do you think that English people are like this? How do you think you would feel if you were English and you read this description?

2 How do the English differ from Americans or Australians or Canadians?

3 Why do some nationalities and races feel superior to others? Is there any real basis for this feeling?

4 Are you proud to be a citizen of your country?

5 What are the main virtues and failings of your nationality?

6 Are national stereotypes valid in any way, or are they merely misleading?

2 Apartheid

3,000,000 whites owned 87% of the land.

8,000,000 blacks owned 13% of the land. (1994)

1926 Colour Bar Act banned Africans from practising skilled trades. Africans were only allowed to be trained to do menial jobs, i.e. to be in constant subordination to the whites.

1936 Africans removed from voters' roll.

1948 Apartheid (literally 'apartness') was imposed. The premise of apartheid was the 'white man must always remain boss'. Supported by the Dutch Reformed Church which gave religious reinforcement to apartheid by suggesting that Afrikaners were God's chosen people and that blacks were a subservient people.

1950 Population and Registration Act authorised the government to officially classify all South Africans according to race; in conjunction with another act, the various races were only allowed to live in certain places. Often resulted in tragic cases where members of the same family were classified differently, all depending on whether one child had a lighter or darker complexion. Where one was allowed to live and work could rest on such absurd distinctions as the curl of one's hair and the size of one's lips.

Education not compulsory for Africans. Less than 50% attended schools. Government spent six times as much on white students than African students.

1953 Reservation of Separate Amenities Act: segregated parks, theatres, restaurants, buses, libraries, waiting rooms, separate post office entrances and other public facilities according to race.

Africans had to carry passes and were not allowed to move freely within the country.

1994 After more than three centuries of rule, the white minority conceded defeat in the elections and turned over power to the black majority.

3 Racial discrimination?

- Instruct students to decide in groups which of the situations they believe are examples of racial discrimination and why. Should the offenders be prevented from what they do and should they be punished? Students may need some help from you in interpreting the situations.

(i) (1) According to the British Race Relations Act (1976) a landlord or landlady who lives on the premises has the right to choose who they want to live in their house.
(2) A director is within their rights to do this.
(3) This horrifying but true story is recounted in Hanif Kureishi's introduction to the filmscript of *My Beautiful Laundrette*. Ask students how they think geography and history should be taught, e.g. in England and America history tends to be taught from the white man's point of view, thus Native Americans may be badly represented in the US, and Indians the same in England. Should we try and teach history from all points of view?
(4) With reference to the 1960s Kureishi had this to say about British TV: 'Television comics used Pakistanis as the butt of their humour. Their jokes were highly political: they contributed to a way of seeing the world. The enjoyed reduction of racial hatred to a joke did two things: it expressed a collective view (which was sanctioned by its being on the BBC), and it was a celebration of contempt in millions of living rooms in England. I was afraid to watch TV because of it; it was too embarrassing, too degrading. The word 'Pakistani' had been made into an insult. It was a word I didn't want used about myself. I couldn't tolerate being myself. The British complained incessantly that the Pakistanis wouldn't assimilate. This meant they wanted the Pakistanis to be exactly like them. But of course then they would have rejected them. The British were doing the assimilating: they assimilated Pakistanis to their world view. They saw them as dirty, ignorant and less than human – worthy of abuse and violence.'
(5) In 1965 the British politician Enoch Powell said with reference to immigrants: 'We should not lose sight of the desirability of achieving a steady flow of voluntary repatriation for the elements which are proving unsuccessful or unassimilable'.
(6) This is known as 'reverse discrimination' and is not permitted by the Race Relations Act. Some years ago a white Englishman applied for the job of gardener at Leicester City Council. He sent off six identical letters. In three he used his own name, and failed, but when he used the name Prakesh Patel, he was granted an interview. He threatened to take the council to an industrial tribunal, but in the end the case was settled out of court.

Writing

- A multicultural and multilingual society is a much healthier society than a one race one language society. Discuss.

4 Language

- Students read the text and then answer the questions in groups.

3 Racial discrimination?

1 A landlady who refuses to let a room in the house where she lives, to a Pakistani girl.

2 A theatre director who will only accept a black actor to play the part of Shakespeare's Othello.

3 A white geography teacher in a predominantly white class who shows pictures of Indian peasants in mud huts, and says, pointing to an Indian boy in the class, 'Hanif comes from India'.

4 A TV producer whose programme contains sketches which ridicule other nationalities.

5 A politician who advocates repatriating all non-white immigrants.

6 A factory that now employs only non-whites on the basis that non-whites have in the past suffered from adverse discrimination and should be given the chance to 'catch up'.

4 Language

Governments throughout the world often use language as a political weapon against ethnic minorities within their borders.

Generally this means that the ethnic language is forbidden from being used in formal situations, such as in schools or legal procedures. Such ideas have even been proposed in California where native-English speakers are frightened of losing their supremacy to Spanish-speaking immigrants. In Britain too, Welsh and Irish political prisoners have been refused permission to speak with visitors in their own languages.

Some minorities rebel, like the Basques in Spain, who use their linguistic differences with Spanish as a reason for becoming an independent state.

Whereas most governments try to discourage the use of ethnic languages, the South African government actually used to encourage them. By denying black Africans the right to learn English, they prevented them from getting positions of power and with communicating with the outside world. ♦

1 Are there any linguistic minorities in your country? How are they treated?

2 Do you have dialects in your country? Who uses them and when? How are they considered?

3 Should all immigrants to a country learn their new country's language? Should they try and preserve their own language? Do you associate people who speak your language badly with ignorance or poverty?

4 Should immigrants or linguistic minorities have the right to have their school lessons taught in their native language?

5 Should the host country try and protect its own language against those of its immigrants, e.g. by making the use of its own language mandatory in all official contexts (e.g. in court, marriage ceremonies, applying for bank loans)?

6 Do people feel more kinship for people who live in the same country as them, or people who speak the same language as them?

YOU

Warm-ups

- Students imagine they are trying to break the ice with a new acquaintance. They have to write down ten questions to ask this person, so that from the answers they can get an overall picture of this person. For students having difficulty in coming up with questions here are a few ideas: best friend, favourite toy as child, most interesting thing they have learned from life, person they admire most, hopes for the future, worst/best day in their life, favourite sport/food/drink/music/book/city etc.

1 You are what you have

- Before students read the text, ask them to write down the four most important things they have. Avoid any questions as to exactly what 'have' means. Most people include four types of possessions: body part or intellect, objects, places and time periods, people and pets. Students then compare their list with their partner's. How did they define 'have'? What did they give preference to? What does this tell them about their personality? Then go straight into the listening.

Listening

- Students hear some people who have just done the above exercise. Students' task is to note down the two people's 'haves', and whether the third person approves of these 'haves' and why.

1 *family, friends, car* **2** *health, friends and cats; approves because they are not materialistic*

A The things I have in my life which are very important to me are my family, my friends and my car. In that order I should think.

B Quite like that one actually.

C Right, the three things important to me are, my health, which I hope is all right, my friends, and my cats.

B I like both these 'haves'; I think I would have gone for something really similar. I think that it's really good that you haven't really put material possessions, especially with yours as your third choice is a car, which obviously is giving you the option of going left right and centre safely hopefully and all things like that, so I completely condone it, and I'm glad you've mentioned your cats.

- Students now read the text and answer the questions in groups.

Follow-up

- In groups, one student takes out the contents of his/her pockets/bag/wallet/case. The other students try to classify these objects and draw some conclusions about the lifestyle and personality of the student. He/She then comments on their observations.

2 Have you ever?

- Students answer questions in pairs or groups.

Listening

- Students listen and match the extracts with the questions a–t.

1 *a* **2** *a* **3** *m* **4** *q* **5** *i* **6** *e* **7** *k*

1 When I was little, when I was little I used to take chocolate or drinks and things out of shops deliberately without paying.

2 I remember particularly one time in Venice with a girlfriend when we ran away from a pizza restaurant after having a huge meal without paying.

3 I've worked in Buckingham Palace so I saw the queen.

4 Well yes, one day I was cycling to work and a scooter came very close to me, and I tried to move over to let them pass. And one of them, the one sitting on the back, a girl, just took, took the bag from my bicycle and raced off into the distance.

5 When I was quite young and we were playing a game and somebody ran in front of me and shut a door with windows in it and I put my hand out to stop the door hitting me and my hand went through the glass.

6 Yes, I've often done that. When we were children we often used to go swimming any time of year.

7 I've never killed an animal bigger than a mouse, but I have killed several mice as my house is out in the country and infested with them.

1 You are what you have

Victims of burglaries often report that they feel they have in some way been personally polluted. This suggests that our possessions are in some way an extension of ourselves. Think of the kinds of things you buy second-hand – you'd have no problem in buying a second-hand car, but second-hand underwear (no matter how clean) you might not even want to touch. Even after we die, possessions may still remain a part of us. This is demonstrated by burial sites, where domestic utensils, jewellery and weapons have often been found. We may even become immortalised in our possessions as they get handed down from one generation to another.

1 To what extent are possessions more important than people?

2 Would you buy something just because it belonged to a famous person?

3 How attached are you to your things? What kind of things would you never lend anyone?

4 What second hand things would you consider buying?

5 Do you have any collections (stamp albums, butterflies, etc.)?

2 Have you ever?

a Left a shop or restaurant without paying.

b Lied about your age.

c Had anything published.

d Had a supernatural experience.

e Swam in the sea in the winter.

f Won a competition.

g Been the victim of a crime.

h Had a holiday romance.

i Broken a window.

j Thought you might be going to die.

k Killed an animal bigger than a mouse.

l Got/Stayed up to see the sun rise.

m Met someone famous.

n Broken or damaged something and not told the owner.

o Got completely drunk.

p Had food poisoning.

q Witnessed a crime.

r Been abroad.

s Forged someone's signature.

t Passed an exam you never thought you'd pass.

3 Would you ever?

- Students answer the questions in pairs or groups.

4 Feelings

- Students answer questions in pairs or groups.

Listening
- Students hear someone doing the same exercise. They have to match the answers with the questions in the exercise.

1 *d* **2** *b* **3** *f* **4** *h* **5** *i* **6** *g* **7** *j*

1 I'd tell them I was there before them.
2 Turn on the radio and try not to get too anxious and nervous; I mean there's nothing you can do about it.
3 A I usually ask someone to explain it to me, which is actually quite often. I obviously don't have much of a sense of humour.
B I wouldn't say that. Odd, maybe, but none at all certainly not.
4 I hate people who arrive late for any situation, and I've ever only been late once in my life for an appointment, and that was because I'd had an accident on the way in, so I was pretty shaken when I arrived; actually it was for a job interview. (And did you get the job?) Yes, I did actually.
5 I suppose I was brought up in a country where some animals are treated as being quite sacred, so it always shocks me when I see someone hitting an animal here. To be honest I don't do anything, I mean, what can you do?
6 A No, I'm not embarrassed at all, and I'm moved pretty easily.
B So you just get out your handkerchief and cry away?
7 Ignore him, if it's a man. Smile back if it's a woman and then think 'why on earth was she smiling at me?'

5 Superlatives

- Students answer questions in pairs or groups.

3 Would you ever ...?

1 Go on holiday alone.

2 Gamble.

3 Kill someone (even in war).

4 Eat raw meat or raw fish.

5 Live in another country.

6 Steal.

7 Buy a very expensive wine.

8 Take drugs.

9 Wear a fur coat.

10 Hit your partner.

4 Feelings

What do you do when ...?

a you can't get to sleep.

b you're stuck in a 10 km motorway queue.

c you're at a party where you know no-one apart from your hosts.

d somebody pushes in front of you in a queue.

e someone is very rude to you.

f you're told a joke which you don't understand.

g you want to cry during a sad scene in a film.

h you're late for an appointment.

i you see someone hitting an animal.

j a stranger smiles at you.

5 Superlatives

1 What's the worst/nicest thing that anyone has ever said to you?

2 What's the best thing that has ever happened to you?

3 What's the most luxurious thing you'd like to own?

4 What are the ugliest/biggest/most unusual/prized/valuable things you have?

5 What's the kindest thing anyone has ever done for you?

6 What's the most embarrassing thing you've ever done/said?

7 What's the worst thing that could ever happen to you?

8 What are the most important things you've learned from life?

9 What's the cruellest thing you've ever done?

10 What's the silliest thing you've ever done?

Zoology

Warm-ups

- Students draw very quickly two domestic and two wild animals (but not easy ones such as giraffes, elephants, snakes, cats, etc.). In small groups they then pass round their drawings and guess what their partner's animals are, giving reasons and commenting: 'it could be a goat', 'it looks a bit like a ...', 'it can't be a bird because it doesn't have wings'. Within the group students compare impressions and then the 'artist' reveals the truth.

- Tell students to write down the names of the first three animals that come into their heads, then three adjectives to describe each animal (i.e. giving a total of nine adjectives). In groups of four tell students to pass their papers to the person on their right. Explain that this is a psychological game. The first animal with the corresponding adjectives describes how they see themselves, the second how they wish they were, and the third how they really are. Each student reads as follows: 'Luca sees himself as a dog, he wishes he were a lion, but he really is a mouse'.

1 Zoos

- After reading the text and answering the questions, brainstorm students on reasons *for* zoos. Then proceed with the listening exercise.

Listening

- Students hear Dr Katz, an advocate of certain kinds of zoos. Students listen and answer these questions.
  Questions: True or false? **1** Dr Katz approves of modern farming methods. **2** Up to 15% of the world's biological diversity may have been lost by the end of the 21st century. **3** Animals are responsible for eating a lot of crops produced by third world farmers. **4** San Diego zoo specialises in breeding endangered species and reintroducing them into their natural environment. **5** Dr Katz agrees that it is better to visit animals in their natural habitat.

1*F* **2***F* **3***F* **4***T* **5***F*

P = presenter I = interviewer K = Dr Katz

P On 'Animal Watch' tonight we'll be dedicating the second half of our programme to the 'Save the whale campaign'. But first I'd like to welcome Dr Alan Katz, a zoo manager, who has joined us tonight to talk about the roles of a modern zoo.

I There's been a lot of criticism been levelled against zoos recently by animal activists who claim that zoos are little more than animal prisons for the benefit of mindless parents with their children.

K Basically such people are taking human rights and trying to apply them to animals, but this precept just doesn't work, at least not with zoos, though I must say I don't agree with some modern farming methods or the breeding of animals exclusively for their furs.

I You mean the conditions of some domestic animals such as chickens and cows, and ...

K Yes, but the point is that zoos are aimed at conservation not incarceration. What man is doing to the animals' natural habitat is terrible; before the end of the next century we may have lost up to 50% of our biological diversity. With the human population expanding dramatically in third world countries, animals are going to be battling for space against farmers trying to produce crops for more and more mouths to eat. The animals will inevitably be the losers and it is one of the zoos' roles to make sure that at least some of these species can be bred in captivity.

I For possible release later?

K Yes, in fact the San Diego zoo, which houses more than 150 endangered species, has returned a dozen of them to the wild. Many animals actually live longer in captivity and raise more young.

I Activists claim it would be better for people to go and see these animals in their natural habitat.

K Ask any ecologist about this and they'd say it would have and in fact already is having disastrous consequences on the environment. Already, organised safaris in Africa are having devastating effects on animals and their environment. Many ecologists in fact would advocate staying at home and watching it all on their TV or computer. But I personally don't see why people can't come to a good well organised zoo, have fun seeing the animals and be educated at the same time, and of course learn respect for nature.

I Thank you Dr Katz.

Writing

- Would you rather be a lion tamer or a lion hunter?

2 The laws of the jungle?

- Students imagine they're members of a civil jury whose job is to sentence the six people in the situations. Decide beforehand what range of sentences can be given, including acquittal. With reference to question **1**, do students think that these types of dogs should be banned from domestic use?

Writing

- Write a letter of protest to one of the following governments: The Chinese/Taiwan governments to get them to suspend trade in powders made from tiger bone (used for quasi medicinal purposes) and rhinoceros horn (aphrodisiac); these have been banned by the UN convention on International Trade in Endangered Species.

Zoology

1 Zoos

Zoos are basically designed for human entertainment; people can learn little or nothing from seeing poor undignified animals forced to go round and round in cages. Tests have shown that penned-up animals suffer unacceptable levels of stress and boredom not to mention physical harm. Those who claim that zoos prevent the extinction of endangered species should ask themselves whether it is really preferable for them to live in such a demeaning and artificial environment than not to live at all.

1. Is the writer for or against zoos?
2. Are all zoos like the one described (i.e. animals in cages)?
3. Do you think it is better for animals to become extinct than to be kept 'artificially' alive in zoos?
4. Do you think that the zoo practice of feeding surplus offspring (i.e. animal babies) to other animals is wrong?
5. Have you ever been to a zoo? How did you feel about the experience?

2 The laws of the jungle?

1. This woman's dog, a rottweiler, savagely mauled and maimed a three-year-old child. This was the second time the dog had attacked a child and on the first occasion the owner had been asked to put the dog to sleep.
2. These animal activists smashed up £200,000 worth of laboratory equipment used by scientists testing animals to produce shampoo.
3. These people trained bears to dance. They drilled a hole through the bear's nose, inserted a chain so that they could pull the bear, and taught it to stand on two feet with the use of burning embers. This practice is illegal in this country.
4. This company bought ivory known to have come from elephants killed by poachers in African national parks.
5. This woman sprayed another woman's £5000 fur coat with red paint.
6. This family abandoned their dog on the motorway before going on their summer holiday.

3 Animal rights

- Before beginning the exercise, brainstorm students on how we mistreat animals. Elicit the following areas: battery hens, bullfighting, cock fighting, force-feeding geese, horse-racing and horse- jumping, circuses, hunting, killing for furs, whaling, etc. In groups, students discuss their attitudes to such activities. Would it be right for the European Parliament to ban bullfighting in Spain? Do we have the right to change other nations' traditions? How much do animals actually suffer? Is keeping a dog in a town apartment any worse than hunting foxes?
- Students now look at the statements on their page and in groups decide whether they are true or false.

ⓘ Pharmaceutical companies wishing to introduce a new drug on to the market have to provide scientific evidence of its safety by getting their drug licensed. This requires toxology testing which in the UK (and many other countries) entails tests on animals. Apparently, 450 million animals are killed for food each year and another 7 million are destroyed as vermin or unwanted pets.

Writing

- Write a letter to a pharmaceutical company asking them to stop testing their products on animals. Then write a reply from the public relations officer of that company.

4 Pets

- Students read the text and answer questions in groups.

3 Animal rights

a

ANIMALS HAVE THE SAME RIGHTS AS HUMANS.

b

Vegetarians shouldn't wear leather shoes, buy leather handbags, and wear fur coats.

c

Other animals eat each other so why shouldn't we eat animals? We're animals too after all.

d

Animals should not be exported: they often stay on board trucks for days at a time, sometimes stuck under the burning sun or in the freezing cold, and nobody even bothers to feed them or give them some water.

e

Through urbanisation, people have become too distanced from animals and thus over-sentimental about them. Hunting used to be necessary for survival, now it is a legitimate form of pest control, and anyway it's an excellent sport.

f

It's better that animals suffer than humans. The list of things that have been achieved through experiments with animals is almost endless: blood transfusions, vaccines, insulin, cancer drugs, organ transplants, the contraceptive pill, treatments for mental illnesses, intensive care for premature babies.

g

Animals don't feel pain like we do.

4 Pets

Love was in the air when Stewart McSkimming met his future wife. But their two pets had other ideas. Quite clearly they hated each other. In the end the snarling stand-off between the dogs didn't prevent Stewart marrying his Josephine. It did get a bit in the way though. The couple decided that there was nothing for it but to live apart while both animals were alive and baring their teeth.

Now Jo's labrador cross, Tanya, has died and the couple's separation will soon be over – almost three years after their wedding. Later this month the 45-year-old artist will leave her coastal bungalow and move 40 miles up the road to move in with Stewart, a dam attendant, and his springer spaniel Gale at their lochside cottage near New Galloway, South West Scotland.

Togetherness should mean an end to astronomical phone bills and the 50,000 miles a year the couple covered for meetings and meals.

'It was awful and pure madness,' admitted Jo yesterday. 'Of course I didn't love Tanya more than Stewart but we couldn't sacrifice the dogs for each other. And because we lived apart, we never took each other for granted. I always used to put my make-up on when Stewart was coming round.'

1. What do you think the journalist's attitude is to this couple?
2. This story was reported in an English national newspaper – does this surprise you?
3. Would you have gone to such lengths for your pet?
4. Which is a better pet – a dog, a cat, a fish, a horse, or a parrot?
5. What kind of animals would you not like to have as pets?

Subject index